Happier than God
rn Ordinary Life into an Extraordinary Experience

Neale Donald Walsch

Cover design by Frame25 Productions
Cover art by John Rawsterne c/o Shutterstock,
Reilly c/o Istock.com, ImageZoo c/o Corbis.com

Emnin Books
PMB 1144
1257 Siskiyou Blvd
Ashland, OR 97520
e-mail: emninbooks@aol.com

ISBN 978-1-57174-576-7 HC
ISBN 978-1-57174-580-4 PB

Distributed by:
Hampton Roads Publishing Company, Inc.
1125 Stoney Ridge Road
Charlottesville, VA 22902

434-296-2772
fax: 434-296-5096
e-mail: hrpc@hrpub.com
www.hrpub.com

10 9 8 7 6 5 4 3 2 1
Printed on acid-free paper in the United States

Happier
than GOD

Turn Ordinary Life into a
Extraordinary Experienc

NEALE DONALD WA

an emnin book

DISTRIBUTED BY

HAMPTON ROADS
PUBLISHING COMPANY, INC

God says for me to tell you this:

Nothing needs fixing;
everything desires A Celebration.
You were made to bend
so that you could discover
all of the many Miracles
at your feet.
You were made to stretch
so that you could find
Your Own Beautiful Face of Heaven

just above

all that you think you must shoulder.

When I appeal to God
to speak to me,
I am feeling just as small
and alone
as you are.
But this is when,
for no good reason at all,

I begin to *Shine*.

(Begin to Shine - © 2007 m. Claire)

TABLE OF CONTENTS

Let us begin with a word of gratitude.

Thank you, God. Thank you for this book and for this life and for the wonder of this moment. Thank you for everything that has ever happened to me, is happening now, and ever will happen. For all of it has produced the perfection of this next breath and the glory of Who I Am now going to be.

Good. Now, on the inside cover, write today's date. You will want to remember it, for you are about to be given a formula for all of life that will change everything in your day-to-day experience.

Unless it does not.

And this is the day on which you will make that decision . . .

CHAPTER 1

You're Now Witnessing an Extraordinary Mechanism

L ife was meant to be happy.
　Do you believe that?
　It's true. I know it doesn't seem like it when
you look around, but it's true. Life was meant to be
happy.

You were meant to be happy. And if you *are*
happy, you were meant to be happier. Even if you're
very happy, you can be even happier.

How happy? Just *how* happy can you be? Well . . .
you can be *happier than God.*

I once heard a lady describing a gentleman who
was very wealthy. She said, "He's got more money
than God!" That's how I mean this. I mean to use
the ultimate superlative.

I also mean the words I have used literally. I
mean just what the words say. Which brings up a lot
of questions. Does this mean that God even *experi-ences* the thing called "happiness"? (Yes.) Does that
mean that God experiences *un*happiness? (No.) If

we can be happier than God, does that mean that we are separate from God? (No.) Then how is this possible?

Well, as it happens there is a *formula* by which you can be happier than God. All mystics have known it, most teachers of mystical wisdom have known it, some contemporary spiritual messengers know it, but it's become, through the centuries, sort of a "mystery formula" . . . because it's not talked about very much. Not very much at all.

Why? Simple. Very few of the folks to whom spiritual teachers and messengers might be talking have been able to believe what the "mystery formula" is said to be able to produce. And when you talk about things that no one believes, you can become very unpopular.

So even today, in what is supposed to be a time of intellectual and spiritual enlightenment, not many teachers and spiritual messengers reveal this formula, even if they know it. Or if they are talking about it, they are talking about only half of it. Most of them are keeping the other half, the most breathtaking part of this formula, under wraps. So what we have here is an amazing truth, but *you don't know the half of it.*

What good is a truth if it's not fully revealed? None at all, of course. In fact, only half a truth can be misleading. It can even be dangerous. So we're going to speak the truth, the whole truth, and nothing but the truth here. We'll start with a look at why you're holding this book, and when we finish, we'll have described an extraordinary mechanism.

Okay? Good. Here goes.

Ask yourself why you picked up this book.

Never mind. I'll tell you. You picked up this book *on an impulse.*

And where did that impulse come from?

You. It came from you.

Why? Why did the impulse originate in you? What caused that to happen? And from what *part* of you did it come?

Those answers take up much of this book—and they're pretty darned exciting. But for now, let's move to an even larger question: How is it that this book just happened to be here—right *here*, where you are, right *now*—for you to even see, much less have an impulse *about*?

Ah, yes, now that is the *key* question. If you knew the answer to *that* question you could change your whole life.

Here's the answer to that question. Get ready to change your whole life.

This book just "happened" to be here, right *here*, right *now*, because *you placed it here*.

You *caused* it to be here.

Okay, look, we're going to explore a lot of things that strain credulity here, so you're going to have to stick with me on this. I told you that the reason that even contemporary spiritual messengers were not coming right out and telling you this is because so few people can believe it, yes? So you get to decide right here. Do you wish to be among them? Or do you want to move past those borders? Do you want to really go exploring? Beyond the reaches of our present ideas and constructions?

If you do, keep turning the pages here and hang onto your seat.

You caused this book to be here, right here, right now. It may not seem as though you did this, but you did.

How?

With quantum physics.

Often people use quantum physics without knowing it. That is, without being *consciously aware of it*.

Quantum physics (read that, *science*, in case you think this is far-fetched) says that "nothing that is observed is unaffected by the observer." If this is true (and it is), then you played a role in all of what is now occurring, exactly as it's occurring. The only question is whether you did this consciously or unconsciously, knowingly or unknowingly, wittingly or unwittingly. But you did do it, I assure you.

You attracted this book to you and you caused yourself to be aware of it and you are now reading it— all out of your deep desire to be happier.

This book made its way from my keyboard to my publishing house to your bookseller to your hands in a way that has nothing to do with accident or coincidence and happenstance.

None of this has occurred by chance.

So be happy. You have just witnessed the most extraordinary mechanism in the Universe. You have just witnessed the *Mechanism of Manifestation*.

Let me put this another way. You have just witnessed . . .

. . . *God, in action.*

(And if that doesn't make you happy, nothing will.)

CHAPTER 2

The Startling Truth that
Will Stun the World

Before we're finished here you're going to receive a lot of clues about how to make yourself happier. We'll talk about specific steps you can take to bring peace to your mind, love to your heart, and joy to your soul—and keep them there.

Intriguing as these steps are, we're not going to discuss them just yet. They will be much more deeply understood, and therefore much more powerful as tools, if they are shared within a larger context.

Outside of that context these steps could seem like just so many other "tips for better living," and this could appear to be just another "self-help" book. It most assuredly is not that. *This book offers a complete explanation of How Life Works.* It can turn ordinary life into an extraordinary experience.

Once you hear that explanation, the steps I referred to above will come alive with meaning. And so I'm going to tell you first about the Process of Personal Creation, about the great Principles of Life, and about that Unspoken Truth.

Back in the sixties there was a bumper sticker that became very popular. It asked: IS GOD DEAD?

The idea behind the question was that humanity had evolved so far so fast that we may have rendered God irrelevant. That thought has been reinforced in recent years with the emergence of teachings on what has been called the Law of Attraction: the purported ability of individuals to *create their own reality* using nothing more than "positive thinking" and "focused intention."

I know, of course, that God is not dead. And most people agree with me. Surveys have shown that the largest percentage of people in every nation and in every culture believe in a power greater than themselves.

Yet if we humans can obtain and acquire anything we want in life using our own power, of what use is a power greater? What would be its function? What would be its purpose?

The astonishing conclusion that many people are reaching, especially given how the "Fast Track to Happiness" is being taught in some circles today, is that we no longer need God.

Now I'm going to say something that, if you believe in God, is going to make you very happy. But not at first. At first, it may make many of you want to put this book down right here. Don't do that, because you're going to miss out on the part that you'll love.

(If you don't believe in God at all, you're going to find what I'm going to say next at the very least intriguing. So hang in there!)

It's true.

We no longer need God.

In fact, we never needed God.

We do not need God for anything.

This is the startling truth that will stun the world. It is the Unspoken Truth that no one wants to utter. Yet this is not all of the Unspoken Truth. The rest of it has to do with *why* we do not need God for anything.

CHAPTER 3

The Promise that Few Can Believe;
The Truth that Few Can Accept

Not needing God is not the same as not having any use for God.

I want to say that twice because it's too important to be glossed over. I said, *not needing God is not the same as not having any use for God.*

In fact, it is precisely because we have an extraordinary *use* for God that we have no *need* for God.

How can we "need" something that we always have, that we cannot *not* have under any circumstances, that we can always use, and that we cannot *not* use no matter how we might deny that we are?

You cannot *not* have God in your life, as part of your life, and this is something that many people cannot believe. They can't believe the highest promise of God: *I am always with you, even unto the end of time.*

You cannot *not* use God, even if you deny that you are, and this is something else that many people cannot believe. They can't accept the most wonderful truth taught by all religions, each in their own way:

Ask and you shall receive.

Because people can't accept this truth, they *completely and utterly misunderstand the formula* by which they can create what they wish to experience in their lives.

I call this formula the Process of Personal Creation—what some people call the "Law of Attraction"—and it does *not* render God obsolete, but exactly the opposite. It makes our experience of God more present, more relevant, and more real than ever.

CHAPTER 4

The New Good News

All great truths begin as blasphemies.

George Bernard Shaw famously said that, and he was right. His observation explains why so many great truths must be very gently introduced, with voices soft and the truths themselves understated.

Yet there comes a time when they can't be understated any longer. They bubble up to life's surface and burst forth in all their glory. These are times of great moment for humanity, for it is through such bursting forth of great truth that our species evolves.

Take the idea that you can be happier than God.

What a thought! What a concept! It's revolutionary! So a lot of people have been resisting it. For years they've been pushing against it, denying it, even making it "wrong."

Yes, people—and, ironically, religions—have been making it *wrong to be even a little happy*, much less happier than God. (Well, maybe they haven't made it wrong to be happy, they've just made it wrong to do most of the things that *make* you happy.)

Many people believe that life was meant to have a lot of pain in it. Suffering should be "offered up" to God. It should be endured in silence. That earns you points in heaven.

Our culture has so completely adopted this idea that some people don't *want* to be happy all the time. When you talk about how you can be "happier than God" they become fidgety, uncomfortable. They warn that you're being "unrealistic." You may even be "trafficking with the devil."

They will tell you that life was *meant* to be unhappy. Life is a trial. It's a school. "No pain, no gain," and all that. People in large numbers believe this. When you say to them that life was *never* meant to be unhappy, that no one has to be unhappy *ever*, they look at you cross-eyed. They don't know what to do with that. They don't know where to go with it. Often, they'll tell *you* where to go with it . . .

Yes, this is blasphemy, this idea that you can be happier than God. Yet it's true. It is not too good to be true, it is too good *not* to be true.

The Good News is that you do not have to go through hell to get to heaven.

Did you hear that? Let that be shouted from every rooftop! Let that be heard from every pulpit and lectern. Let the word go forth from this time and place: *Happiness is your natural state of being*, and you can occupy that space all of the time. You never have to be unhappy again.

This does not mean that you'll never be sad again, but sadness and unhappiness are not the same thing. We're going to explore that here, as we look deeply at how you can be happy all the time.

Am I happy all the time? No. I'd by lying if I said I was. Am I happy more of the time than ever before? Yes. Is this starting to feel like *most* of the time? Yes. Do I really think I can be happy *all* of the time? Yes.

And you can be, too. You can be *happier than God*.

None of this involves materialism, or "me-first-ism." In fact, the formula doesn't work that way. The formula does allow you to create anything and everything you want, and I know that sounds like materialism, but once you know the *whole* formula, once you hear the Unspoken Truth in full, you'll be very clear.

So let's start with a basic truth, and then we'll get to the truth *behind* the truth . . . more of that *Unspoken* Truth.

The basic truth was given to you in the first six words of this book.

Life was meant to be happy.

I asked you then, and I'll ask you now: Do you believe that? If you don't, then life will have no choice but to play itself out according to your non-belief. Don't be surprised if you are unhappy more of the time than you would wish. Yet if you believe that life *was* meant to be happy, it will be.

Now you may be thinking, *Really? Then how do you explain all the pain in the world, and all the suffering?*

Fair question. And before we're through here, you'll have an answer. But right now, just for now, please focus on the six-word statement with which this book began. Let's see if it can be embraced as at least a *possibility*.

CHAPTER 5

When Seeing Is Not Believing

I am saying here that it is possible that *believing* your life can be happy most of the time *can make it so*. Yet that's old news. We've all heard that before.

This book is about what you *haven't* heard. It's about an even larger truth that is behind this truth. A truth so large, so . . . how shall I put this? . . . *alien to our experience and to everything we have been taught* . . . that, as I have twice already noted, many people cannot believe it even when they *see* it. When they see this truth come to life right in front of them *they attribute it to something else.*

There's an old saying that "seeing is believing," but let me tell you about Magellan's Ship.

I learned about this from my dear friend Stephen Simon, who produced and directed *Conversations with God: The Movie* and *Indigo*, co-produced *What Dreams May Come*, and is responsible for many other films you may have heard of, such as *Bill and Ted's Excellent Adventure.*

As Stephen explains it, Magellan and his men explored many islands and did so without opposition from the natives living there, who might have been expected to climb into their dugout canoes and launch a full-scale attack on these strange looking sailors as dangerous interlopers, but instead welcomed them with open arms. The reason? When native lookouts first spotted Magellan's ship, *they didn't know what they were looking at.*

They had never seen anything so huge and so majestic carrying people on water before. The gigantic ships, with their enormous masts and sails fully billowed, were so far outside of the experience of these island natives that they had no point of reference from which to even begin to consider what these vessels might be. They anchored their canoes, laid down their spears in awe, and welcomed Magellan and his men as gods.

Stephen told me this is the Magellan's Ship Syndrome—a phenomenon that occurs when what one is looking at is so far from one's experience, that person literally doesn't know what to make of it.

Well, the Unspoken Truth I have been referring to here is so far removed from anything that most of us have ever been taught or told that even when it plays its effect in our lives, producing a direct manifestation right in front of our face, *we literally don't know what we're looking at.* We'll see one thing and call it another.

We'll see the outfall of the Unspoken Truth and call it the product of coincidence or serendipity or accident or chance . . . or just plain dumb luck.

In fact, there will have been nothing "dumb" about it, but just the opposite: the workings of the highest intelligence in the universe.

CHAPTER 6

The Most Important
Question Ever Asked

The exciting journey of the mind that follows may very well be the most important exploration you will take in your life. That is why you brought yourself here. That is why you had the impulse to pick up this book. Everything here you already know. You just don't know that you know it. Or maybe you do, and you're just having a hard time remembering it. Or maybe you even remember it, but are having a hard time *applying it.*

If you see yourself in any of those categories, you are going to benefit enormously from the clarity that you are going to bring yourself here—having used the *Mechanism of Manifestation* to *tell* yourself about the *Mechanism of Manifestation*.

That mechanism is what we are going to be exploring. In my own vocabulary I call this the power behind Personal Creation. It has to do with *how things come about.* It has to do with how reality *becomes* reality.

Now I've already said, just a bit earlier, what some of you may already be thinking: "Oh, *that* stuff. Yeah, I've heard all that before. Didn't they just make a movie about that?"

They sure did. But they didn't mention the Unspoken Truth hardly at all. As it always does in discussions about manifestation and creation, this truth behind the truth darned near got lost, because it went largely unspoken. Who wants to be marginalized as a blasphemer?

But it's time that we spoke of this hidden truth. I mean all of us, not just some of us; all of the spiritual authors and teachers and speakers and messengers who would seek to address the question of How Life Works.

It's one thing to say that we can all be happy, that we can all experience whatever we choose in life, and that we all have the power to create our own reality, *but it's another thing to tell us why.*

We've heard a lot about *how* Personal Creation works, we've heard a lot about the *way* it works, but we've hardly heard anything at all about the *reason* that it works.

This has led to a lot of questions—and one in particular that might just be the most important question of all time.

I've had this question asked at my lectures and spiritual renewal retreats often. Other messengers have heard it too, I'm sure. And now it's been asked on global television.

When this question is answered fully and completely you will know how to be *happier than God*.

During a February 2007 telecast of *Oprah!* a member of the studio audience asked it and almost stopped the show. The broadcast was devoted to that motion picture that was capturing a lot of attention at the time, having to do with the so-called "Law of Attraction." This "law" is a phenomenon which has been described in the books and programs, classes, and lectures, statements, and sermons of many teachers and messengers throughout the centuries. On her worldwide telecast, Oprah used these words to describe this great principle of life:

"It says that the energy and the thoughts and the feelings that you put out into the world, both good and bad, are exactly what is always coming back to you...so you have the life that *you* have created. I've been talking about this for years on this show . . ."

Oprah's on-set guests were waxing enthusiastic about using positive thoughts and feelings, consciously and deliberately to bring about desired results in one's life as described in the film, which was called *The Secret*, when Oprah called on a woman in the audience who, she said, "has a question that many people want answered."

The woman then rose to say . . .

"My husband and I, we are Christians, and our kids are Christians. We teach our children to put their faith in God, and it seems that *The Secret* teaches you to put your faith in yourself. So I was wondering if God is anywhere in this."

Oprah thought that was a good question, and I can understand why. Since we were children, most of us have been told that God is the One to whom we can turn if we need help, or if we desire something that is really important.

Isn't that how millions of us have been trained? No matter what the culture, no matter what the religion, if a person believes in a Deity at all, isn't this one of the most important roles that the Deity plays? Is God not the supplier of all good things?

Yet what of the dramatic assertion in some teachings and writings that if we need a miracle or wish better health or want more money or ache for a perfect companion or seek right livelihood or simply desire a better life, all we have to do is use the power that lies within us, "speak our word," and everything for which we yearn will be ours?

We must ask again, where *does* God fit into all this? If what was said earlier—that we don't "need" God because God is always with us—is true, then just *how does God fit into all this?* What is God's role in the Process of Personal Creation?

CHAPTER 7

The Work of the Devil
or the Work of God?

I n order to understand how Personal Creation *increases* rather than *decreases* God's role in our lives, we must know everything there is to know about the *Mechanism of Manifestation.* We must have that mechanism thoroughly explained to us, as well as the principles of life which support it.

The Process of Personal Creation is actually three phenomena interacting as One. The first phenomenon has to do with God, the second has to do with you, and the third has to do with you and God together.

Another way of describing this would be that Part One of the "mystery formula of life" is the *I Am,* Part Two is the *You Are,* and Part Three is the *How To.*

The fact that all three of these aspects are not deeply understood by most people is why the principle of "attraction" has been called a "secret."

Some people have said they've tried using this principle and have thought it to be ineffective, disappointing, and disheartening. I believe that is because these people are working with only part of the data.

Others want nothing to do with attraction or Personal Creation no matter how much data they have, feeling that it may actually be "evil"—the work of a devil who seeks to lure us away from our reliance on God by seducing our egos with thoughts of our own power.

And religious traditionalists are not the only ones who might shy away from this process. The list includes many of those who are simply seeking to live God-centered lives and experience a personal relationship with the Divine (whether inside or outside a traditional religion). Not all of these people may be comfortable with the claim that they, themselves, are solely in charge of creating their own reality.

Then there are also non-religious rationalists who believe that what cannot be explained by evidence, reason, and logic is *irrational* and can only lead to self-delusion.

The fact is that nothing within Personal Creation is evil *or* irrational. But, as I have said, much about that process has not been sufficiently explained.

Until now.

CHAPTER 8

A Tool with Two Handles

A s more and more people around the world are exploring the possibility that they, themselves, have the power to deliberately create whatever they choose, I think it will be highly beneficial to just take a breath here and look at . . .

1. *Why* Personal Creation works.

2. *What* we might use it for other than bringing ourselves more money, bigger houses, new cars, or more sparkling jewelry.

3. *How* Personal Creation is reconciled with all the pain and suffering in the world, and how it can be effective in alleviating that pain.

We are talking here about power, folks. We are talking here about huge amounts of power. But so much has been said and written about this power that as I began thinking about this book I found myself wondering, is this text really necessary? Will it really be helpful?

Then, just as I was about to drop the project, I happened to see, on an Internet bookseller's site, a critical reader review of the way in which "positive thinking" and Personal Creation is taught by some.

Said this particular reader, in part:

> *I have been interested in the power of the mind for many years now . . . (but) I am so offended at the "get rich" aspect . . . that we all just have to focus on having a new car, money and mansions and it will happen. Some of my greatest lessons in gratitude have come from realizing I have enough now.*
>
> *I believe we should use our positive thoughts to find meaning in the existence we already have and to enrich our spiritual lives. Doubtless, positive thoughts and believing you are worthy of love and abundance will open you up to receive more of the same, but it is not some kind of magic spell and it is not a secret . . .*
>
> *Positive thinking can help you envision succeeding and make you open to new opportunities, but it won't magically pay your bills.*
>
> *By far the most offensive part of the message is the suggestion that people who have pain in their lives are somehow attracting it with their thoughts. Darfur rape*

victims did not ask for it. Children who are molested did not ask for it. Starving Africans did not ask for it.

To suggest that their "incorrect thinking" is the cause of this is sickening . . .

I was astonished to come across these words just as I was about to abandon this book as a bad idea. It was as if the universe was yelling at me: *Don't abandon the book!* I knew then that if I dropped the project, far too much would be left to misunderstanding, misinterpretation, and mistaken notions of the most important and wonderful aspect of human life.

There are those who are now saying that the way Personal Creation is currently being taught has taken a wonderful gift out of a sacred treasure chest and placed it in a store window. They are saying that the touting of "attraction" and "manifestation" as a means of personal enrichment and the satisfaction of personal desires could, in fact, take people to a place of material abundance, but it might leave them in spiritual poverty.

While I know that most contemporary teachers of creation theory come from a very spiritual base, I think we all need to hear this critique and not simply write it off as having no validity.

I think we need to add more substance to our communications about the Process of Personal Creation so that those who hear of it can move to a place of richer, fuller, deeper awareness with regard to it.

Here is some substance that I would like to add: Personal Creation (and the Energy of Attraction that is so integral to it) is a product of Divine Love.

Personal Creation is about the *power of life to produce more life*. It is about power, plain and simple. The power to change your life.

"Attraction" is a gift from a benevolent and compassionate Deity. It is a tool with two handles—one in God's hands and one in ours.

That tool is in your hands right now. What you think of these words, right here, right now, will empower them or disempower them, and will empower you or disempower you.

Your thought about this very paragraph will create your experience of it. If you think that this is all nonsense, then it *will* be in your reality. If you think that this is true, then it *will* be in your reality. It is as simple as that.

Your ideas about the rest of this book, and about the Energy of Attraction, will be no different. This principle is part of the Process of Personal Creation, a power that is waiting to be wielded, waiting to be used, *consciously* rather than unconsciously (which is how it is now being used by most of humanity). Like all tools, it is most effective when it is used for the purpose for which it was intended.

I want you not to miss the enormous implication of all that has just been said.

I have just said that that "attraction" is a *tool*, that this tool was created by God, and that the tool has been given to *us* to use *with God*.

I have also said that it is *most effective* when used for the purpose *for which it was intended.* (And so we see another reason why some people who have used Personal Creation have thought it to be ineffective, disappointing, and disheartening. They are not using "attraction" for the purpose for which it was intended.)

And just what is that purpose?

It is to create a happy, peaceful, joyous life for everyone whose life you touch, and for you, in that order.

Please take note of those last three words. They will change everything you thought you understood about the Process of Personal Creation and the "mystery formula" behind How Life Works.

CHAPTER 9

The Great Principles of Life

The ability to create your reality is an expression of Divinity. That is why it always works. It is impossible for it *not* to work. It is a fundamental principle of the universe. It is *the nature of things.*

I said a moment ago that "attraction" is a tool that works *most effectively* when it is used for the purpose for which it was intended. That is, it most often produces *the results that are desired* when it is used as it was designed to be used. But it is always producing *some* result because it is *always being used*—whether those using it know that or not.

This is the great gift of God: Continuous Power, Continuously On.

We are talking here about a systematic process of cause-and-effect that never shuts down.

God *is* that process. God *is* that system. This is what God means when God says to us, "I am with you always, even unto the end of time."

That is something that is not generally understood, and that is rarely explained, about God. It is almost *never* explained in relation to the topic of Personal Creation.

We need to now contextualize this business of "attraction."

The Energy of Attraction is part of a *larger system of cause-and-effect in the Universe.*

Talking about "attraction" as if it were a law unto itself is a little like talking about the gravity without discussing the physics explaining what gravity does, and why. Okay, so a thing drops. So what . . . ?

Let us look, then, and look deeply, at the great principles of life.

Life expresses itself through:

1. *The Energy of Attraction*, which gives you power.

2. *The Law of Opposites*, which gives you opportunity.

3. *The Gift of Wisdom*, which gives you discernment.

4. *The Joy of Wonder*, which gives you imagination.

5. *The Presence of Cycles*, which gives you eternity.

This larger system regulates the Process of Personal Creation. You might even call this system, and this process, "God."

This is a new thought to many people. Invite yourself to explore this idea, just for now. Could "God" really be, after all is said and done, a *process?* And could that process be the experience called Life? Is the Process of Personal Creation simply the playing out of life as it naturally expresses?

Life, I have come to understand, is God. It is God *being* God, and becoming what God is next going to Be. This is a complex and extraordinary system that includes a *Process* that produces an *Expression* called life.

This system is a circle. Imagine this circle in your mind. On this circle, life's *process* produces life's *expression*, life's *expression* creates life's *experience*, and life's *experience* creates life's *process*. One thing leads to another, which leads to another, which leads to another, in a never-ending cycle. It is all One.

Life as it is created is the process, life as it appears is the expression, and life as it affects us is the experience. *How* it affects us is determined by us—and this is not something that is understood by most people.

The eternal cycle of process/expression/experience is Divinity Itself. It is God, *godding.*

This is the manifestation of the Presence of Cycles. All things respond to this presence. All things exist in cycles. All things have their being within the system—and there is nothing outside of that system.

Attraction is part of this system, as are the other great Principles of Life. Conscious *use* of the Principles that are the foundation of the Process of Personal Creation produces an Expression of life that leads to the Experience of Divinity.

Are you tracking me here? Stay close to me. Keep tracking. Re-read a few words if you wish to. Keep tracking.

Now . . . just as physics explains and controls the physical aspects and elements of our lives, so, too, does metaphysics explain and control the larger-than-physical aspects and elements of our lives.

Attraction is part of those metaphysics. It is an *energy magnet.* It pulls to itself everything like itself. It obeys, absolutely, the principle: Like Attracts Like.

This energy magnet, this Power from God, is being used by us in the Process of Personal Creation—and it is being used all the time, whether we are aware of it or not, whether we acknowledge it or not.

So now, when discussing our own power to produce our own reality, we never again have to ask, "Where is God in all of this?"

Now we know.

CHAPTER 10

Conscious versus Unconscious Choice

I t is because the system never shuts down, it is because the power that God has given us is always *on*, that it sometimes *looks* as if the Process of Personal Creation is not working.

Let me say something once again, just to be clear. Personal Creation is *always* working.

Earlier I observed that some people have tried using the Personal Creation process and have thought it to be ineffective. Personal Creation is *never* ineffective, although it does not always produce the results that we desire. It is precisely because it *is* so effective that it does not do so.

The Energy of Attraction, you see, responds not only to what we desire, but also to what we fear. Not only to what we wish to draw to us, but also to what we wish to push away. Not only to what we consciously choose, but also to what we unconsciously select.

"Selecting" from what my friend Deepak Chopra calls "the Field of Infinite Possibilities" is a delicate procedure. It is a matter of what we focus on, *whether we want to or not*, whether we do it *consciously or not.*

For instance, if your mind is focused on doubling your income within the next year, but if you have a later thought, the next hour or the next day, that it will be almost impossible for you to do this—if you say to yourself, "Oh, come on, be practical! Pick a goal that you can at least *reach*"—then you have selected the latest idea, *whether you originally wanted to or not*, because the switch on your power is always *on*; Personal Creation is always working.

It not only works with your most recent thought or idea, but also with the one to which you give the most frequency and focus and emotional energy.

This explains why some people who seek to use the process to get something they desperately want often meet up with what they call failure. Then they say, "See? This stuff doesn't work!"

Actually, the process is working perfectly. If you experience yourself wanting something desperately, and if you keep saying to yourself *I want that!*, you are announcing to the universe that you do not now have it.

(Unless you are simply using the word "want" as a figure of speech. Most people are not. When most people say that they "want" something, they are very clear that it is because they experience that they do not now have it.)

As long as you hold such a thought, you *cannot* have it, because you cannot experience on the one hand what you are confirming on the other that you do *not*.

To use one example, the statement "I want more money" may not draw money to you, but may actually push it away. This is because the universe has only one response in its vocabulary: "Yes." It listens to you very carefully, and it listens most of all *to what you are feeling*.

Conversations with God says that "feeling is the language of the soul." If you constantly say, "I want more money!", and the Universe "feels your feeling" around that, and it is a feeling of lack, *this is what the universe will respond to.*

We are talking about *power* here. The power of a magnet. Remember that a feeling is *energy*, and in the matter of energy, Like Attracts Like. So the Universe will say "Yes!"—and you will continue *wanting more money.*

If you think, "I want more love in my life!", the universe will say "Yes!"—and you will continue *wanting more love in your life*.

In using the Energy of Attraction, the word "I" is the ignition key of creation. What follows the word "I" *turns* the key and starts the engine of manifestation.

Thus, when it "looks as if" Personal Creation is not working, it is only because the Energy of Attraction has brought you what you *inadvertently selected* rather than what you thought you chose.

If the power were not always ON, if the process was not always working, you could have a single very positive thought about something and that outcome would be made manifest in your reality without fail. But the process works all the time, not just part of the time, and is fed by that which you feel most deeply, most consistently. So a single very positive thought in a whirlwind of not-so-positive ideas and projections is not likely to produce the desired result.

The trick is to stay positive in a sea of negativity. The trick is to know that the process is working even when it *looks as if* it is not. I want to give you now an implement with which to do this. It is an incredible technique. It works every time.

CHAPTER 11

The Miracle that Will Change Your Life

S taying positive when surrounded by—even when *submerged in*—what others might call "negativity" is easier than you think. The trick is to bring an end to judgment, to "judge not by appearances."

When you bring an end to judgment, you bring an end to an entire way of living. This is no small thing. This is a life changing shift in attitude and behavior. This is a miracle.

But how does one perform this miracle? That is the question to which everyone wants an answer. Please, then, pay very close attention to what I am going to tell you now: The way to move *out* of judgment is to move *into* gratitude.

That is such an important corollary that it should be plastered all over your house and everywhere in your world. On your bathroom mirror. On the refrigerator door. On your car's rear-view mirror. Above your computer screen. You might even tattoo it on your left wrist—or at least engrave it on a bracelet that you wear there:

The way to move out of judgment is to move into gratitude.

This means remaining grateful for every out-come. *Every* outcome. This is about saying "Thank you, God" for even those things that you are sure you did not consciously choose and that you are very clear you do not want.

Somebody once said, "Happiness is not getting what you want, it is wanting what you get." That "somebody" was profoundly right.

Gratitude is the miracle cure for every moment of dis-ease. It is the fastest way to dissolve anxiety, to heal disappointment, to replace negativity with positivity. It is the shortest route from a dead-end back to The Path. It is the *connecting energy* to God.

Try it some time.

The next time you are confronted with any unde-sired outcome, result, or experience, just stop. Stop right in the middle of whatever's going on. Just . . .

. . . stop.

Close your eyes for the smallest moment and say inside your head, "Thank you, God."

Take one good, deep breath and say it again.

"Thank you for this gift, and the treasure that it holds for me."

Be assured that it *does* hold a treasure, even if you are not seeing it right now. Life will prove that to you, if you give it a chance.

———

When gratitude replaces judgment, peace spreads throughout your body, gentleness embraces your soul, wisdom fills your mind. Let gratitude replace judgment and your whole experience of life will take a turn for the better in five seconds.

In five seconds.

This is because attitude is everything. Attitude puts the course correction in life when you have stepped off The Path. Attitude is like the Map of the Mind. It is like the Global Positioning Satellite of the brain.

A negative attitude will send you down the road to unhappiness. There is no avoiding it. It will absolutely happen, and it doesn't matter what the problem. A positive attitude will put you back on The Path to inner peace and happiness. Again, there is no avoiding it. It will absolutely happen, and it doesn't matter what the problem.

Yet how can one move into gratitude when the circumstances or conditions presenting themselves are utterly miserable, desolate—or even life threatening?

By knowing that every moment in life is an unparalleled opportunity for you to inwardly declare, express and experience the Divinity that lies within you.

This is something that is not made clear by a simple announcement that there is such a thing as the Energy of Attraction. That fact must be *explained*, not merely *revealed*.

CHAPTER 12

Why Life Becomes Contrary

I nadvertent Selection is just one little known aspect of Personal Creation that can cause people to think it's not working. There is also the Law of Opposites, about which people know even less, and which produces the same effect as Inadvertent Selection, but for a different reason.

The Law of Opposites is the second of the five great Principles of Life and it works in perfect harmony with the Energy of Attraction. This principle states that no sooner will you call something into your reality than its exact opposite will also appear—and always *first*.

What is this now? What am I saying?

I am saying that the moment you choose anything—any outcome, object, or experience—the *exact opposite* of that will come into your life in some way. It may show itself in some far distant quarter, or it may pop up right in front of your eyes, but it will be there, absolutely.

It is *necessary* for the "opposite" of whatever you are choosing to create with the Energy of Attraction to show up, for the reason that *life cannot be experienced in a vacuum.* A *context* must be produced in which you may experience what you have chosen.

Because not many people know this, they can easily turn negative in their thinking just when the universe was preparing to place before them all that their hearts desired.

They do not see the appearance of the opposite as a sure and certain sign that they are on the right path, heading toward their chosen objective. Rather, they see it as an obstacle, a blockage.

They experience themselves to be up against the wall, when really they are standing in front of a doorway. Only *discernment* would allow them to know the difference. This is where the Gift of Wisdom comes in (which will be explored momentarily).

The Law of Opposites is based on the *fundamental and founding principle of all life*: "In the absence of that which you are not, that which you are is not."

I know, I know, that's not a very clear sentence. Let me clarify. Let's say, for the purposes of illustration, that you wish to experience yourself as "the light." (Many people, by the way, have actually chosen this. They wish to be The Light—and thus to bring The Light—wherever they are, wherever they appear.)

Now let us imagine for the purposes of this illustration that there is nothing else around you *but* The Light—indeed, that there is nothing else in *existence* but The Light. This would make it impossible to experience yourself *as* The Light. You may "know" yourself as that, but you cannot "experience" yourself as that.

(There is a difference between knowing and experiencing, and it is *experiencing what it knows itself to be* for which the soul yearns.)

There is only one way to experience yourself as The Light, and that would be to find yourself in darkness. Yet remember, in this example there *is* no "darkness." In this illustration, there is nothing but The Light. You, therefore, *must create the darkness.* You must *call it forth.* And you will.

This is the Law of Opposites, which gives you opportunity. Yet if you see the opposite not as opportunity but as opposition, you will see it not as something that empowers you, but as something that takes power away from you. You will fall into negative thinking, not understanding that you, yourself, have used the Energy of Attraction to draw to you the darkness as *well* as the light (what you would call "negative," as well as what you would call "positive," outcomes) in order to *fully experience* the positive outcomes that you are creating.

There is *power* in opposites, and this is the intricate way in which attraction works with all the great principles of life. Those principles work in concert with each other; they function as a perfect mechanism—the *Mechanism of Manifestation*—like gears in a finely tuned watch.

What are we to do, then, when the Law of Opposites seems to be thwarting, rather than supporting, Personal Creation?

Understand exactly what is going on.

Endeavor to see the appearance of the "opposite" as your first indication that Personal Creation is working flawlessly. Remember that the *first step* in creating anything is creating a *context within which it may be experienced.* Do not resist the opposite of anything that you wish to experience. Instead, embrace it. Look right at it and see it for what it is.

What you resist, persists. That is because, by your continued attention to it in a negative way, you continue to place it there. You cannot resist something that is not there. When you resist something, you *place it there.* By focusing angry or frustrated energy on it, you actually give it more life.

This is why all great masters have urged us to "resist not evil." Do not *fight* that which is opposite to your stated desire or your preferred outcome. Rather, relax into it.

I know that may sound strange, but I promise you, it works. Do not become rigid and tense, ready for a *battle. Never oppose that which opposes you.* Do not OPpose, COMpose.

Do you understand? Remember this little rule always:

Do not oppose, compose.

Compose your original idea of how you want life to show up. And compose *yourself* while you're at it. Come from a place of relaxed assurance that life is functioning perfectly. Yet do not confuse relaxation with acceptance.

"Resist not evil" does not mean that you should not try to change what it is that you do not choose. Changing something is not resisting something, it is merely choosing again. Change is not resistance, but alteration. To modify is not to resist, but rather, to continue Personal Creation.

Modification *is* creation. Resistance is the *end* of creation. It firmly holds the previous creation in place.

Do you see?

At every moment of difficulty and challenge in your life you have a choice: opposition or composition. To repeat: You can either oppose that which you are experiencing, or compose that which you chose.

Compose what you chose.

Now, thanks to the Law of Opposites, you have a *context* within which to experience it. And that is the greatest thing the universe could ever give you.

This is an important aspect of the "mystery formula" of life that is rarely explained.

And there is still more.

Chapter 13

The Way Out of the Negativity Trap

When the Energy of Attraction responds to the Law of Opposites, the Gift of Wisdom may be used to add *discernment* to the experience.

This principle states that: "All wisdom lies within you. You have not been put on the earth by a merciless God who chose not to give you the wisdom to know how to function in this environment. Quite to the contrary, you were put here to *use* this environment in order to achieve the purpose for which you came—which is the purpose of Life Itself—and you were given the wisdom to understand both the purpose *and how to achieve it*."

Call on this wisdom whenever and wherever you feel the need for its guidance. It will be there.

Wisdom is a tool given you and all sentient beings. The Gift of Wisdom gives you discernment. It is what allows you to see that any negative experiences you may be undergoing have been brought *to* you *by* you as you build a Contextual Field within which you may experience what you have chosen to experience of yourself and your world.

Often this "work" is being done at a subconscious or superconscious level. Thus, you may not be consciously aware of it. The Gift of Wisdom makes it possible for you to be consciously aware, to emerge from the Cloud of Unknowing, to move with clarity through the Contextual Field that is life around you, and to invoke the Energy of Attraction *within* that Contextual Field, focusing consistently on exactly what it is you now choose, and recognizing all contrary conditions as also your creations, producing opportunity, not opposition.

Masters have said to us, "Judge not by appearances." This is what they have meant.

Discernment allows you to see things as they really are and not fall prey to SATAN (Seeing Any Thing As Negative).

The Gift of Wisdom allows you to know that as you journey along the path of life you can *expect* what some people call "failure" along the way.

"The more thou dost advance, the more thy feet pitfalls will meet," Helena Petrova Blavatsky tells us. "The Path that leadeth on is lighted by one fire—the light of daring burning in the heart. The more one dares, the more he shall obtain. The more he fears, the more that light shall pale."

The trick is to see "failure" for what it is. Not failure at all, but opportunity.

I like Joseph Sugarman on this:

> "Not many people are willing to give failure a second opportunity. They fail once and it's all over. The bitter pill of failure is often more than most people can handle. If you're willing to accept failure and learn from it, if you're willing to consider failure as a blessing in disguise and bounce back, you've got the potential of harnessing one of the most powerful success forces.
>
> "Each problem has hidden in it an opportunity so powerful that it literally dwarfs the problem. The greatest success stories were created by people who recognized a problem and turned it into an opportunity."

This is what I call really using the Gift of Wisdom, opening yourself to discernment and allowing yourself to see the difference between appearances and reality, noticing that what appears to be negative is in reality positive.

It is through true Wisdom that we understand something quite extraordinary about life in physical form: all of physicality is an illusion.

Conversations with God makes this statement repeatedly, and if it is true, we have to know how to deal with that.

God says that we are like magicians who have forgotten our own tricks. We are living in an *Alice in Wonderland* world, where we swear that what is "so" is "not so," and that what is "not so" is "so." Yet, the fact that we *are* living in an illusion is what makes our lives so exciting, and their possibilities so endless. For only in a fantasy can we have anything we want, and do anything we please, and create anything we desire.

Lewis Carroll wrote:

"There is no use trying," said Alice, "one can't believe impossible things."

"I dare say you haven't had much practice," said the Queen. "Why, I believe six impossible things before breakfast!"

The trick in all this, of course, is to know how to live *with* the Illusion, and not *within* it. Or, as the Bible says it, to be "in this world, but not of it." There is a way to do this, and in the CwG book

Communion with God, we are given that way in the Triad Process of Reality Creation.

Says *Communion with God*:

The Master, and the student on the journey to mastery, *knows* that the Illusions are illusions, decides why they are there, and then consciously *creates* what will be experienced next within the self through the Illusions.

When facing any life experience there is a formula, a process, through which every person may move toward mastery. Simply make the following statements:

1. Nothing in this world is real.

2. The meaning of everything is the meaning I give it.

3. I am who I say I am, and my experience is what I say it is.

This is how to work with the Illusions of Life.

The first step in the Triad Process is, for many people, the most difficult. It proclaims that everything we look at, everything we experience, is unreal. Nothing is actually what we imagine it to be.

This *does not mean that it is not there.* What it *does* mean is that it is not "real." That is, it is not "really" what it "looks like." It is not what we assume it to be.

For greater insight into this phenomenon, I suggest reading *The Holographic Universe,* by Michael Talbot. This extraordinary book brings us insight, from a scientific point of view, into the make-believe world in which we live.

The statement "Nothing in this world is real" is based in quantum physics – yet it is more than a scientific observation. It is a psychological and spiritual truth as well (a deeply spiritual perspective on this idea will be found in *A Course in Miracles,* which states: "Nothing I see is real"). Awareness of this truth can be very healing—particularly in times of great trouble or great stress.

If you think that what you are experiencing during times of difficulty is real, you will quite literally *make it real* in terms of the effect that it has in your life. If, on the other hand, you know that it is unreal and that its effect is simply something you are making up, having no sum or substance whatsoever, you can *disappear that effect* in a single moment.

Conversations with God says that what you resist persists, and what you look at disappears. That is, it ceases to have its illusory form.

Now if you are thinking that this is very much along the lines of the message of the science fiction movie *The Matrix*, you are absolutely right. You will remember that, in that film, the characters were depicted as living in a make-believe world, created by their thoughts, and that the lead character, Neo, became a sort of "god" among men by simply training his mind to resist the appearance of things (such as bullets coming at him) and deny their reality.

By literally denying the reality of anything that is now happening to you that you do not wish to have happening, you are, at the very least, going to reduce its negative effects. Dr. Norman Vincent Peale, a popular Christian minister in the 1940's and 50's, pointed this out in his extraordinary book of fifty years ago, *The Power of Positive Thinking.* So did author James Allen in his classic, *As a Man Thinketh.*

Of course, the master teacher Jesus said it directly and perfectly when he declared, "As you believe, so will it be done unto you."

So the first step in the Triad Process is one of denying the reality of the internal effect on you of *anything.* This means the so-called "good" as well as the so-called "evil." Now, "what is the point of denying the so-called 'good' effects?," you may ask.

The answer is that, by looking straight into the face of your greatest joy and calling it what it is—an illusion—you fail to become deeply attached to it. You may continue to enjoy it, but you literally "enjoy the hell out of it." That is, you remove the hell of becoming addicted to your enjoyment of life in one particular form.

It is addiction—to people, to places, and to things—that creates agitation where once there was peace, misery where once there was joy, pain where once there was pleasure, sorrow where once there was happiness. This has never been more clearly described than in the deeply insightful book by Ken Keyes Jr., *A Handbook to Higher Consciousness*. That book—written by a paraplegic who spent his days in a wheelchair—changed my life forever. It says that you can tell that you are addicted to a person, place, or experience if the absence of that person, place, or experience causes you to lose your happiness.

Published some years ago, *A Handbook to Higher Consciousness* is still available today. It teaches how to elevate "addictions" to "preferences," and I consider it one of the most extraordinarily insightful books ever written on the subject of human happiness.

It is important to note that by denying the ultimate reality of everything we think, say, and see, we are not necessarily sending it away from us. We are merely re-contextualizing our *experience* of it, causing ourselves to notice that what we are looking at is an illusion. Only then can we empower ourselves to either (a) allow the illusion to continue, or (b) create the illusion as coming to an end.

So long as we think that what we are experiencing is real, we will imagine ourselves to have no such power to change its effect on us. We will see ourselves as powerless in Life itself, simply moving through the experience and constantly being at the Effect of it.

Denying the ultimate reality of all that we see is, therefore, an extremely powerful and important tool in the Process of Personal Creation.

Now we are ready for Step 2. If nothing I see is real, then what does anything mean? That's another very good and fair question, and the answer is: *The meaning of everything is the meaning you give it.*

This second step puts you firmly in command of your experience. You may not have changed anything in your outward reality, but remember, it is the *experience* of it that we are out to change.

You, and you alone, decide what anything means to you. You, and you alone, get to choose what matters and doesn't matter, what is "good" and what is "bad," what is "okay" and what is "not okay." You, and you alone, get to determine whether you are going to react positively about something or negatively about something—or, interestingly, have no reaction at all. Your emotions are entirely under your control. Your feelings are what you want them to be.

"That's not true!" you may protest. "I don't *want* to feel bad, I just *do*." Yet this is not so—and the sooner you understand this, the sooner you will move to mastery in your daily living. You *do* want to feel bad or you wouldn't. The trick is to look deeply into the moment to see *why* you want to feel bad. The answer to that question unlocks everything.

To reiterate, *you* decide, and you *alone* decide, what something means to you, and how you are going to respond to it. Yet this is a decision that most people make based upon past feelings, experiences, understandings and desires, or future fears, apprehensions, wishes or desires.

None of this has anything to do with what is going on right here, right now.

The idea, as Eckhart Tolle made so brilliantly clear in *The Power of NOW,* is to *stay in the moment.* Don't "futurize" and don't "pasteurize." I have come to see the real power in this in my own life.

When I "come from yesterday," I frequently overlay meanings on things that are happening right now that are not in those things *inherently,* but that I have *placed there* as a result of a previous thought

about them—or about something similar to them—
from my past. (Going to the dentist might be a good
example.)

When I "come from tomorrow," I overlay an
idea about some imagined future (and usually some
imagined fear) on the events of today. These future
realities may never come to pass (in fact, my life has
shown that they rarely do), but what they often do
is ruin any chance I had to maximally profit from the
experience of the moment.

Only when I get *out* of my past and stay *away*
from my future can I genuinely experience what's
happening right here, right now, within the context
of just that: what's actually occurring *in the present
moment*. And—free from the interpretations of the
Past and the Future—I can give that occurrence *any
interpretation I desire*.

This was the greatest liberating lesson of my
life. When I learned this, I understood at last that *my
experience of everything that is going on, is going on in
my mind.* I can stare into the face of events and I can
choose to *be* whatever I wish to *be* with regard to
them. I can be "okay" or I can choose to be "not
okay." I can be "happy" or I can choose to be
"unhappy." I can be "optimistic" or "fearful," "powerful" or "powerless," "complete" or "incomplete,"
"destroyed" or "reignited."

The decision is all mine. The meaning of everything is the meaning I give it.

In the third step of the Triad Process of Personal Creation I decide that I am who I say I am, and my experience is what I say it is. This may all seem circular, but there is a method to the madness.

I have a vivid memory of a woman who spoke up once at one of our Foundation's ReCreating Yourself retreats. She had been sexually abused as a child by her uncle, and she spoke about it in very calm terms. She spoke also about a woman's support group that she had attended on a regular basis, and remembered how, when she told that group about her experience, its members raised their voices in concern. "You should be furious about this!" they told her. "How can you speak so calmly?"

"Well," she had said, "that was a long time ago, and besides, I understand why he did what he did, and I've forgiven him. So I'm not angry anymore."

"Not angry anymore?" they protested. *"How could you be not angry anymore? Don't you know what happened to you?"* Then they told her that she had apparently "sublimated" her feelings and buried her rage, and was angrier than she knew. "A walking time bomb," they called her. The only problem was, she didn't feel that way. Her experience is what she said that it was, and she became unwilling to "buy

into" the way others in her group told her that she was supposed to be feeling.

I never forgot this example of Personal Creation. The exterior experience of this woman was no different from the experience of many other women who have been abused as a child, but her *interior* experience was remarkably different. She simply chose to hold the experience in another way.

In my own life, when something crazy or unwanted happens, I never ask myself, "Now, why did *that* happen . . . ?" Rather, I ask myself, "If I could *give* that a reason for happening, what would it be?"

I *assign* everything a reason, rather than looking for one. And I *decide* how I am going to feel about things, rather than looking to see how I feel. And I *choose with great deliberation* my responses to everything, rather than watching my responses from the sidelines as if I was not the major player in my life.

The Triad Process of Personal Creation is what I call a Turn Around Process. That is, it is one of those teachings that, once internalized and utilized, can turn around one's entire life.

CHAPTER 14

Life as an Extraordinary Adventure

After using the Gift of Wisdom to see what is opposing you (nothing) and what is inviting you (everything), you may apply the Joy of Wonder. This formula states:

"All things are filled with wonder, for wonder is the Nature of God, the essence of Divinity, and your natural state of being. Enter into the wonder that you are, and from that place of wonder imagine your future, your life, and your collective reality in the next grandest version of the greatest vision you ever held about Who You Are. In this you spread wonder throughout your world and achieve the purpose for which you *came* to the world."

The Joy of Wonder gives you imagination, allowing you to take all that you have drawn to you through the Energy of Attraction and the Law of Opposites and permitting you to produce your experience of this in all the creative ways that only a rich imagination could conjure.

Life becomes an extraordinary adventure when you use the Energy of Attraction, the Law of

Opposites, the Gift of Wisdom, and the Joy of Wonder to magnetize, contextualize, discern, and select that which you wish to experience right here, right now.

Your life on earth, as it is being created right now, is the result of this. If you do not like any part of what you have created, individually or collectively, you may recreate it anew . . . in the next grandest version of the greatest vision ever you held about Who You Are.

The larger the creation, the more power will be required to modify it. If we are talking about you being hungry, you can modify that creation relatively easily. If we are talking about world hunger, it will take more power (that is, more of *you*) to alter the creation, to recreate it anew.

This is something most humans have been to date unwilling to do. These and other non-beneficial worldwide conditions, all created by humanity, exist not because they cannot be changed, but because there has not been the collective will to do so.

Where there is a will, there is a way.

Whether it is in the collective lives of humanity or in your own individual life wherein which negative conditions have prevailed, you need not feel eternally discouraged.

CHAPTER 15

Do Not Worry, You Have Forever

After invoking the Joy of Wonder and allowing yourself to express life in the way that you have, you may find it beneficial to observe and honor the Presence of Cycles.

This fifth great Principle of Life states: "All of life moves in cycles. There is no straight line in the universe. Everything ultimately curves in on itself. The line may be trillions of miles long—or unfathomably *longer*—but everything ultimately meets itself. The movement of energy and mass around this oval creates the experience of what you would call Infinity. This means you have 'forever' to experience that which you wish to experience of Who You Are, individually and collectively."

Everything in life moves in a swirl. Life itself is a cycle, with no start and no finish. Everything exists "as it was in the beginning, is now, and ever shall be, world without end." The Presence of Cycles gives you the gift of eternity.

Does that mean there is no reason to do anything about conditions here and now? Yes and no. There is no reason at all if you are satisfied with the way you are experiencing your life and life around you, if life accurately represents you and the highest idea you have about yourself.

If, on the other hand, you are not satisfied, and if you wish to use this present lifetime for the purpose for which it was intended, then you may choose to alter individual and collective conditions presenting themselves in your life.

It's up to you. You are doing something very sacred here, something very daring, during your life upon the earth. You are defining yourself, and then recreating yourself anew, in each golden moment of Now.

Every act is an act of self-definition.

This includes the act of doing nothing . . .

———————

Some statements were made earlier that I want to get back to before they are forgotten without having been fully explained.

I said that when people have used the Process of Personal Creation and thought it to be ineffective, disappointing, and disheartening, it is because they were not using the "attraction," which fuels the creation process, for the purpose for which it was intended.

I then said that its purpose is to create a happy, peaceful, joyous life for everyone whose life you touch, and for you, in that order.

Finally, I said that those last three words would change your understanding of Personal Creation forever.

This is the most important aspect of Personal Creation, and it is the least discussed.

Because it is discussed so little, critics of Personal Creation and the use of "attraction" have had a field day suggesting that it encourages behavior that is selfish and self-directed, self-serving and self-aggrandizing, and therefore has little to do with goodliness or Godliness.

Yet the *purpose* of the "attraction" (and of all of the great Principles of Life) is to elevate not the Self, but the Other, to expand not the Self, but the Other, to enrich not the Self, but the Other—for it is by *so doing* that the Self is elevated, expanded, enriched, and experienced most fully.

(It is this fullest experience of the Self for which the soul yearns. This is, in fact, the purpose of all life.)

This focus on the Other is not emphasized by many contemporary teachers of Personal Creation, but it is the focus of every ancient spiritual master—*and that is why it looks to some as if Personal Creation and the Energy of Attraction are not in concert with traditional religious teaching.*

There are really only two basic questions to ask in life:

1. What can I give to another?
2. What can I give to myself?

It is important to *never reverse the order of the questions.*

It's okay to ask what you can give to yourself. In fact, it's very okay. Personal ambition, personal happiness, personal fulfillment, and personal spiritual development stoke the fires of desire, of yearning, and of achievement. They are the cornerstones of evolution.

It's very natural and not at all spiritually inappropriate to seek a particular outcome, or to wish for a particular experience, on a personal level—including the experience of wealth, fame, and power. These

are among the gifts of life, they are among the enjoy-
ments of being human, and there is nothing wrong
with them. Yet the process by which we seek to
achieve them is important.

Obviously, achieving these things at the
expense of others is not spiritually evolved. Not so
obviously, achieving these things while ignoring others, and the needs of others, is the hardest way to get
where you want to be going. It is the toughest path.
It is the slowest, most difficult route.

The Energy of Attraction always works fastest
when we ask life's Two Basic Questions in their original order. When the questions are kept in that order,
the first question always answers the second.

This aspect of Personal Creation is stated in
another, perhaps more direct, way in the
Conversations with God series of books. It is these
books upon which the information here is based. As
some of you may know, I am the author of these
texts, and they changed my entire understanding of
life and how it works. They contain the "mystery
formula." They contain the Unspoken Truth.

In the beginning of the *CwG* dialogue I was
desperate to know: "What does it take to make life
work? Why does my life have to be such a continuing struggle?" I shouted inside my head: "Tell me the

rules! Somebody, just tell me the rules! I'll play, I promise. *Just give me the Rule Book.*"

In the nine extraordinary dialogue books that followed, God did exactly that. And in answer to the questions above God said (and I am paraphrasing here, for brevity):

"Your life does *not* have to be such a continuing struggle. The problem is simple. You think your life is about you. Your life is not about you."

"It isn't?" I asked.

"No," God answered.

"Well, then who in the world is it about?"

"*Everyone* in the world."

CHAPTER 16

Here It Is: The Unspoken Truth

T hat little statement—"Your life is not about you"—changed my life. It turned everything upside-down. Or, more accurately, right side up.

I was not here to serve myself, I was told. I was here to serve others. It would be in losing myself that I would find myself. And it would be through giving that I would receive.

This sounded immediately familiar to me. It had the ring of standard Christian doctrine and, for that matter, of the basic teaching of all the world's great religions.

It turns out that it *is* the teaching of religions, but there is something that most religions don't include in this teaching. They don't say *why* this teaching is true. They don't say *why* this process works. *They don't explain Personal Creation.*

My conversations with God made it all clear to me. This process works and it is the fastest way to achieve *anything* one seeks to achieve, God told me, "because you are the Only One In The Room."

I didn't understand. I said something like, "Huh?"

God explained:

"All things are One Thing. There is only One Thing, and All Things are part of the One Thing That Is.

"Therefore, what you do for another, you do for yourself; and what you fail to do for another, you fail to do for yourself."

The reverse is also true. What you do for yourself, you do for another; and what you fail to do for yourself, you fail to do for another. (That is why it has so often been said, "If you cannot love yourself, you cannot love another.")

But now comes a *huge* part of the "mystery formula" for how life works. Now comes . . .

The Multiplier Effect.

By focusing on yourself you limit the amount of energy that you output, because *there is only one of you*. Yet by focusing on others you *multiply* the amount of energy you output by the number of others with whom you do so.

This is something that no one ever explained to me before. Now that I see it, it makes perfect sense to me. If everything is energy (and it is), and if energy creates (and it does), then the more energy you use, the more quickly and magnificently you will create!

And everything that you create, you experience. This is because, ultimately, all things that proceed *from* you come back *to* you. And *this* is because there is "no one else in the room." There is no one *but you*, in multiple form. The very first spiritual principle revealed in *Conversations with God* is: "We Are All One."

Until I understood this and began working to heal all others, I, myself, would be slow in healing—for if part of Me was not healed, how could I be healed completely? Until I understood this and chose genuinely to love all others, I, myself, would be slow in being loved—for if part of Me was not loved, how could I be loved completely? Until I understood this and sought earnestly to remember all others as Who They Really Are, I, myself, would be slow in remembering Who I Really Am—for if part of Me was not remembered, how could I be remembered completely?

The Whole of Us must be known in order for any part of us to be Whole.

We are a hologram.

Therefore, do unto others as you would have it done unto you. For what you do unto others *is* being done unto you—for the simple reason that *there are no "others."* There is naught but You.

You are an Individuated Aspect of Divinity Itself. And this has not been said very loudly, or very often, for this is the ultimate blasphemy.

The fear is that if this is said too loudly, too often, the acceptance that some people have given to Personal Creation will be lost. For the one truth that humanity has found the most difficult to accept is the one truth that would free humanity forever.

It is the Unspoken Truth:

God and We Are One.

CHAPTER 17

You Have No Need to Worry about Yourself

The Unspoken Truth is a direct challenge to every idea that most people hold about themselves—to say nothing about the idea they hold about God. It is also *central* to the question of *how things come about*. It has *more than anything else* to do with how reality *becomes* reality.

Understanding (to say nothing of teaching) the Process of Personal Creation requires us to talk a lot about God. It may also be beneficial to talk a lot *to* God.

I have done so in my conversations with God, and some of what I'm going to say in this chapter will be found in my previous books detailing those conversations. If you've read one or more of those books, what follows will be familiar. Please indulge me, on behalf of those who have *not* read those earlier writings. (And note that there is no harm in revisiting these insights.)

As I've said on several occasions now, many messengers who would tell others about the "Law of Attraction" seldom mention the word "God." I believe this is because some of those writers and filmmakers may feel that the idea of God being the source of the Energy of Attraction takes away from the main point they wish to make—which is that the power lies within *you*.

It seems clear that some of these messengers have made the assessment that, for the general public, an explanation that puts the Process of Personal Creation in people's own hands is what it will find most exciting. Make people feel *powerful*, some for the first time ever, and you've given them a great gift.

I do not disagree with that one bit. Yet I believe that if you do not bring "God" into the Process of Personal Creation, you'll be tempted to think that you are the *sole* power behind the process—instead of thinking that you and God, in partnership, are the *soul* power behind the process. If you fall to this temptation, I am certain that you will be enormously less effective in manifesting what you wish to create.

Personal Creation is God's way of saying to us, "Your will is My command."

This is a difficult thing for many people to accept. It's a very challenging way for many people to think of God. Most people who believe in God at all think of God as commanding *us*. They do not see us as commanding God. Yet God *does* say to every human being, "Your will is My command."

This is true not because God is magnanimous, but because God is ubiquitous; not because of the enormity of God's love, but because of the enormity of God Itself.

God is so big that there is no place that God is not. This is another stunning truth about life that many people do not fully understand—and that so many religions do not *help* people fully understand.

Many humans think that God is *limited* in some ways. They believe that there are some places that God is not. They also believe that there are some things that God cannot control. Both of these ideas are inaccurate.

Let's look first at this matter of control.

You could not lift your little finger if God did not want you to. Therefore, everything that you are doing—indeed, everything that has happened on the earth—lies inside, not outside, the Will of God.

There are those who say that this or that is "not God's Will." Yet if something were not God's Will, how could it happen?

There are those who say that God *allows* it to happen. Yet if God allows it, would that not then make it God's Will? Can a thing that God permits be said to be a thing that God does not *wish* to permit? Yet if God *wishes to*, does God not *will to?* What is the difference between God's "wish" and God's "will"?

Everything is God's Will, and that is proven by the fact that it is happening. This must be true...unless we truly are Children of a Lesser God.

———

Just as God is not limited in terms of power, so is God not limited in terms of size. God is, as noted, *ubiquitous*. God is everywhere. That means there is no place that God is not.

No place.

This idea is theologically revolutionary. It announces God's ever-present reality in, and as part of, all things.

Including you.

Many people believe that God is everywhere, but do not believe that God resides inside of them. They may say this out of humility, but actually it is the height of arrogance to imagine that God exists everywhere in the Universe *except in you.*

That would make your body, mind, and soul pretty exclusive real estate.

If we accept, on the other hand, what even tra-ditional religions say: that God is the Alpha and the

Omega, the beginning and the end, the All-In-All, then we must necessarily conclude that God exists in us.

This is a big conclusion, because if it is accurate (and it is), we come upon a most intriguing and significant inquiry: *Where* in us does God exist? In our little finger? In our big toe? In our brain? In our heart? In our soul? (Do we even have a soul?) (Yes.)

The answer: if God really *is* the All-In-All, the Alpha and the Omega, then there can be *nowhere* in us that God is *not*. In fact, there is nowhere in *anything* that God is not. God is everywhere, and is made manifest in everything.

This brings us back to the Unspoken Truth. If God is everywhere in you, if there is nowhere in you that God is not, then God is *you*.

And everything *else*.

Once you understand this, you cannot imagine that life is about "you" ever again. Not in the sense of "you" having to be, do, or have anything in particular in order to be happy. Not in the sense of you "needing" anything, or requiring anything, in order to survive.

Living in this truth makes it extremely difficult to get "caught up" in the minor daily "dramas" of life as it is currently lived by most people on the earth, and provides a fresh perspective on the really major tragedies and turmoil of our species.

For 50 years I lived a case of mistaken identity. I thought I was separate from God. Now I know that this is not true, and that God and I are One. This does not mean that "I am God" in the arrogant sense of those words. This means that "I am what God is, and God is what I am." This means that I truly *have* been made in the image and likeness of God!

And so have you.

On a strictly personal level, this means that you have no need for anything at all, and so you can drop all of your personal day-to-day "dramas" right now. Since you *are* everything you could ever imagine that you need or desire, what is there to be agitated about?

You desire love? You *are* love. You desire abundance? You *are* abundance. You desire compassion, forgiveness, understanding? You *are* compassion, forgiveness, understanding.

You may not experience that you are these things if you have been living a case of mistaken identity, yet the fastest way to experience that you are these things is to be these things. And the fastest way to experience yourself being these things is to give these things away. For it is in the giving that you realize and multiply the having, and it is in the having that you experience and expand the being, and it is in the being that you embrace and express the knowing of Who You Are—and this is the purpose of all of life.

So don't go around asking, *What are we to eat? What are we to drink? Wherewithal shall we clothe ourselves?* Seek ye first the kingdom of God and all else will be added unto you.

Do not worry about you. Your life will be taken care of. Worry about everyone whose life you touch who doesn't know this.

Conversations with God makes it very clear that your survival is never in question, and the final *CwG* dialogue book, *Home With God in a Life That Never Ends*, redoubles that message, bringing it forward with unqualified specificity, explaining exactly what is going on during the eternal journey of the soul.

This conversation tells us that Life itself is an endless loop, and that the energy of life is everywhere present, individuating as you and me and everything that is. The individuated aspects of Divinity (what we call "souls") travel along this endless loop, from the realm of the absolute to the realm of the relative and back again, from spirituality to physicality and back again, over and over through all time, which is only one time: the only moment there is (which we call Now).

The purpose of this continuing journey is to create an eternal opportunity and an infinite context within which we may experience and express, become and fulfill, know and recreate Who We Are.

We seek to know ourselves as that which is Divine, in all of the aspects of Divinity Itself, and we are using Eternity and Infinity as our tools with which to do that. Eternity and Infinity are God's greatest gifts.

How can the journey be eternal? Simple. When we reach the "end" (defined as the ultimate and total knowing and experiencing of Who We Really Are), we simply do, as a Whole, what we have been doing as individuated aspects of Divinity: we recreate Ourself anew in the next grandest version of the greatest vision ever we held about Who We Are. We then individuate once again, and use the process of life once more to experience that next grandest version, piece by piece.

My final dialogue with God gives us a glimpse into that process, and how the great Principles of Life work. Here, from the text of *Home with God:*

In this holy trinity—God in three parts—your mind is where your conscious activity takes place. Therefore, think only what you choose to experience, say only what you choose to make real, and use your mind to consciously instruct your body to do only what you choose to demonstrate as your highest reality. This is how you create at the conscious level.

Look at this closely. Is this not what every master has done? Has any master done more? No. In a word, no.

Chapter 18

Why We Forget, and How

Chapter 13

Why the ... Bird Flew

The more we become, the more we are capable of becoming, and the more we are capable of becoming, the more we become. Were it not so, life would ultimately and logically come to an end, for growth would come to an end, and when growth stops, life stops, for the process of life is growth itself.

Life will always become a larger version of Itself. And when the largest version of Itself is realized, known, and experienced, Life will invent an even larger version. For Life has no intention of ending. God has no intention of not being God. It could not even if It wanted to. The one and only thing that God cannot do is Not Be.

This is the one thing that you cannot do, either. But you can do something quite unusual. You can *forget who you are.* And, indeed, you *will* do this, in order that you may experience Who You Are again. In order to experience that you are Divine.

Why is forgetfulness necessary? It is really quite simple. God is the Creator. This means that you are the Creator. Yet for you to experience yourself as The Creator you would have to create something, and everything that there is to create has already been created. Everything that ever was, is now, and ever shall be, *is now.* Time is an invention of God, allowing you to see all that has been created *one thing at a time.*

For you to experience yourself "creating" something, you would have to not be able to see everything at once. *That is why time was invented.* Since at any given "point" in "time" you cannot see everything at once, you cannot know that everything has already been created.

. . . unless, of course, you happen to *remember* that this is so.

This is where forgetfulness comes in.

Time creates the possibility of Memory. (In the place of no-time, "memory" is both impossible and pointless, as everything is perceived at once, right here, right now.)

Memory, like time, is limited. Eternity is not. It is timeless. Because both memory and time are limited, and because that which is limited cannot hold that which is unlimited, you cannot hold in human memory a knowledge of all the things which have been created in all the when/where's of eternity.

Memory is limited to "then" and "there," whereas Here and Now is not limited at all, but extends forever through eternity and infinity. Even in your own earthly experience, notice that it is *always Here and Now.* There is *no other time at all* that you can experience!

Are you tracking this? Stay close to me here. Stay close.

Godliness, it turns out, is a One-Time Experience.

God wishes to experience Godself *always.* Indeed, forever and ever, and even forevermore. And so God invented *you.*

You and time and everything in life are God's tools, allowing God to experience Itself endlessly. Through the devices of time and memory, which produce the possibility of forgetfulness, you are able to experience *creating again.* This act of recreation is God's Great Joy. That is why it is called "recreation."

When you, as a human being, "create" something of out thin air (which is, of course, how everything has been created, since everything created by humans was once merely an idea in someone's mind), all you are really doing is "remembering" that it already exists.

All things already exist. All effects, all circumstances, all outcomes—all conceivable experiences and expressions of life—have already occurred and now exist in Timeless Space. They rest peacefully in all the when/where's of eternity (to use Robert Heinlein's memorable phrase).

What you are doing when you use the Energy of Attraction is to magnetize and call forth, from the Field of Infinite Possibilities, the experience and the expression of life that you choose right here, right now.

In this you once again experience being a creator. And you can "create" (call forth) virtually anything you choose. You simply have to know how the "choosing" is done.

CHAPTER 19

A Word about "Negative Thinking"

There are those who say that the Process of Personal Creation allows nothing "negative" to be thought, observed, or spoken. I can understand how some people could come to this conclusion, but the conclusion itself is erroneous.

No one who teaches Personal Creation through positive thinking would suggest for a moment that not a single thought may be given to existing conditions that do not suit your sense of who you are and who you choose to be.

Proponents of positive thinking discourage negative thinking, true, but they do not discourage *any thinking at all.* And observation is not negation. It is simply observation. "It looks like it may rain today," "I can hear the train coming," "Four children die every hour on this planet from starvation," are not negative comments. That is not throwing "negative energy" around. That is simply saying what is so.

How can you do anything about "what is so" if you can't even *say* what is so? Well, of course, you can't. So the doctrine of positive thinking does not require you to close your eyes and ears to the world. It does not require you to become a Pollyanna, calling everything wonderful, no matter how horrible it is.

Calling everything "perfect" is not the same as calling everything "wonderful." Calling a condition perfect is simply acknowledging that it exists in exact alignment with your soul's in-this-moment agenda—which may very well be to *change* the condition as a means of knowing, demonstrating, and experiencing Who You Really Are.

It is, therefore, very okay to observe previously created conditions, circumstances, or possibilities that do not please you, to take responsibility for your role in co-creating them, to speak a word of gratitude for their existence, and then to choose again, creating another condition or circumstance, without judgment or condemnation. ("Judge not, and neither condemn.")

Proponents of positive thinking may say, with regard to any so-called negative aspect of your life, "don't give it a second thought," but they would never say, "don't give it a *first* thought."

Certainly you have to be aware of the world around you—the world that you and others collectively co-created in times and places preceding this particular when/where. The admonition is simply not to *dwell* on those things you do not choose, but no one said not to *observe* them.

Telling yourself that you are living in a world of your highest choice in every moment is not what positive thinkers are suggesting. Knowing that you can *bring about* a higher choice if you truly wish to do so is what positive thinking is all about.

Living in the knowing that the world is "perfect" (ideally suited to your individual, and humanity's collective, agenda) in the moment that you and others create it, and knowing that you may draw up a new definition of perfection any time that you wish, is living in mastery.

And you *can* draw up that new definition and create that new reality at any time that you wish. Individually, this is possible in the moment that you change your mind about anything. Collectively, this is possible when collective consciousness shifts. As with individual consciousness, it is possible for collective consciousness to shift in any single moment.

The opportunity extended to every member of the human race is to be at cause in the matter.

You really are the creator of your own reality, and we are creating together the reality being experienced by the lot of us. Using the power of God-in-us, we are completely in charge here.

This is the Unspoken Truth, spoken fully.

CHAPTER 20

The True Nature of God

Early in this text I said that the Process of Personal Creation is actually three phenomena interacting as One. The first phenomenon has to do with God, the second has to do with you, and the third has to do with you and God together.

I said that another way of describing this would be that Part One of the "mystery formula of life" is the *I Am*, Part Two is the *You Are*, and Part Three is the *How To*.

The tendency among many humans is to conceive of God—the *I Am*—in a way that *reduces* rather than *recognizes* God's power. If we are not careful, we will find ourselves more interested in experiencing God as an *image* rather than as a *power*.

We are now going to learn more about the power of the *I Am*.

When we finally come to the conclusion that God is not simply a larger version of humans, complete with all the emotional turmoil, complexities and needs of human beings (the need for love, the desire for revenge, etc.), we then come to the whole of the Unspoken Truth: God is not a larger version of humans, *humans* are a smaller version of *God*.

This is where the road to total comprehension of life's biggest mystery begins—because this is part of the mystery itself.

Surely the biggest mystery throughout the ages has been God's identity. Yet this has not been a mystery because God has wanted to keep it a mystery. This has been a mystery because *humanity* has wanted to keep it a mystery.

(Or, at least, certain portions of humanity.)

There has been a huge investment within our species in continuing to think of God in particular ways or images. Most people do think of God as a sort of giant human; a massively more powerful and infinitely wiser "Us." Many humans and human religions have even given God a gender (male, in most recent millennia) and a race (definitely not black). That is, *some* humans have. Others have given God different characteristics.

It is said that not many people actually believe any of these ideas, but that such thoughts are better than nothing. The mind needs something it can hang on to, something it can conceptualize and visualize. Yet if people don't believe these things literally, what, then, *do* they believe?

If they were honest, I think most people would tell you they don't know *what* to believe when it comes to the exact nature or appearance or characteristic of God.

I love to tell the story of the six-year-old girl sitting at the kitchen table busily at work with paper and crayons.

Touched by the scene, her mother, caught up in her own work at the sink, sang out across the room, "What'cha drawing, pumpkin?"

"God," the child responded matter-of-factly.

"Oh, honey, that's so sweet," her mommy smiled, "but you know, nobody really knows what God looks like."

"Well," the little girl chirped, "if you'll just let me *finish* . . ."

In March of 2007 I delivered a *satsang* in Tokyo in which I discussed God's true identity. Early in the program I described God in this way:

"God is not a Super Being in the Sky, with the same proclivities and emotional needs as human beings, including the need for love and for revenge. God is life's Essential Energy. You might want to call that energy Pure Intelligence.

"Intelligence doesn't care whether you believe in It or not. It doesn't care whether you use It on purpose or not. If you do use It on purpose, It doesn't care *how*. It makes no judgment about any of this. In fact, It makes no judgment about anything at all.

"Pure Intelligence wants nothing, needs nothing, seeks nothing. It simply Is. It exists in a way that allows Itself to be used. It does this, it allows this, it makes this possible, by placing Itself inside of Everything.

"Wherever you look you will find Pure Intelligence. It is at the basis of all things that exist. Snowflakes reflect Pure Intelligence. The tiniest atoms reflect Pure Intelligence. The biggest swath of the night sky reflects Pure Intelligence. The process of life Itself, examined at every level, reflects Pure Intelligence.

"The energy that I am here calling Pure Intelligence can be used—is being used—at every level of life, by Life Itself. You are using this energy, you are focusing this energy, every second of every minute of every hour of every day . . . usually without knowing it.

"The fact that this energy exists, and the way to focus it, therefore using it to one's personal advantage, is what has been called 'the secret.' A movie by that very name was made last year and is now sweeping across the world.

"This energy that I am calling Pure Intelligence, and that I am telling you is another name for God, has no opinion about anything. That is because It doesn't need anything. It is singularly *without* need, for the simple reason that it is *everything that exists in any form whatsoever*. This includes not only physical things, but metaphysical things as well. This includes all spiritual things, and anything in any form that simply IS . . . including thoughts, emotions, feelings, ideas, and, yes, the black holes of space.

"Think about this. If God is truly everything that exists in any form whatsoever, what in the world could God want or need or require? Why would God punish us for not giving God what we imagine that God wants or needs or requires?

"The answer to these questions is self-evident. It need not be discussed in great detail, because simple logic reveals it to us and makes it clear how we have been held captive by the mythologies of our own culture and its past.

"The opportunity that lies before us, and before all sentient beings, is to use the Essential Energy of Pure Intelligence in the way in which it was designed to be used. Not all things that exist in the universe can use this Essential Energy consciously. That is, with full self-awareness and with intention. Only those elements of Life Itself that are self-conscious—that is, aware of themselves—can do so.

"I should correct that last statement. Not even all elements of life that are self-conscious can use the Essential Energy consciously. It is not only a question of being conscious, it is also a question of the *level* of consciousness that a being or a species has attained. For instance, a dog, while highly intelligent, is not sufficiently self-aware (as far as we know) to be able to use Essential Energy with intention.

"Human beings are not only aware of themselves, they are *aware* that they are aware, and so have risen to at least the Second Level of Consciousness. This level of consciousness allows sentient beings to notice themselves, and even to notice themselves noticing themselves. That is, we can stand 'outside of ourselves' and watch ourselves doing what we are doing and thinking what we are thinking and saying what we are saying.

"We can even watch ourselves watching ourselves. We can step back into the hallway of awareness, looking through doorways both forward and backward — and, according to some, ultimately seeing and experiencing our Divine and Sacred Self."

As I concluded the above remarks, I thought I had been fairly "safe" in my definition of God (I left the part about God being *us* for later in the discussion), so I wasn't ready for someone in my audience to plunge into despair as a result of my description— but I see now that I should have guessed this might happen.

CHAPTER 21

Your Total Freedom Is
God's Greatest Gift

Wh hen I finished with my comments at that *satsang* in Tokyo a man in the back of the room rose to ask what he said was a burning question.

"When I first read *Conversations with God* I was very touched because it allowed me to believe in a God who was personal, a God who loved me. Now I am confused. You have just described a God who is not even a person or a being, and who doesn't care what I do or how my life turns out.

"I feel desolate after hearing this description from you. This is not what I came expecting to hear today. It is very depressing. Can you help me?"

It was a marvelous question. A question from someone who was tracking every word and weighing every nuance and implication. Others in the audience nodded their approval and added, with their eagerly uplifted faces, to the thrust of the inquiry. I shifted my weight from one foot to the other, cleared my throat, and began to speak in a slow, steady voice, the words coming from somewhere beyond my conscious mind.

"The fact that God is Pure Intelligence does not preclude the possibility of God taking the form of a sentient Being. In fact, if Pure Intelligence is the essential energy of All That Is, then it can presumably take the form of any part of that. In other words, 'God' can 'show up' in our lives in any form that is desired.

"So what we call 'God' can continue to shape Itself as a Being that looks very human, if this is how It feels that It would be most understood or most easily embraced in any particular moment by any particular Individuated Aspect of Itself.

"Indeed, I have come to understand that the energy that is God takes the form of exactly what and who God is showing up for. And so it is that, for human beings, God takes the form of a human being.

"Yet God is not *limited* to that form. Indeed, God can 'show up' *in any form that we wish*—including pure, undifferentiated energy—and we can shape that undifferentiated energy into anything that we choose.

"How? By using the Process of Personal Creation!"

Now the audience perked up. Suddenly, the pieces were beginning to come together.

"Before we go on with that," I said, "let's talk about this business of God not caring, and the idea that this means God is not loving.

"Not caring what we do is not the same as not loving us. I want you to imagine your own children, sent out to the back yard to play. Do you care what games they choose? Does it matter to you whether they play Tag or Hide and Seek or Kick the Can? Of course not. In fact, you would never even dream of impinging on their inventiveness by dictating to them how they must use their play time.

"All you say to them is, 'Go, now, and play! Enjoy yourself! But be careful. Try not to hurt yourself! And *if you need me, I'll be right here.*'

"This is what God says to us. The fact that God does not care what we do is a sign of how *much* God loves us, not how little! For *freedom* to be and do and have what we choose is the greatest joy of all. It is the biggest treasure and the grandest gift that God could give us. Even traditional religion teaches that God has given us this gift. It is called Free Will."

Again, nods of recognition and understanding rippled through the audience. You could see that people were "getting it." Things were coming together in their mind.

"Now, getting back to the Ultimate Nature of God . . . I said that God can 'show up' in any form that we wish God to show up in—including an old man with a beard, a ray of golden light, or pure, undifferentiated energy—just as *we* can shape into anything that *we* choose.

"We can, you know. It's just that we do it one cell at a time and that which we call God does it all at once.

"Recently medical science has come to understand more and more of what are called 'stem cells.' Do you know what stem cells are? They are cells in the body that have no particular characteristic whatsoever. But they can *adopt* characteristics by renewing themselves through cell division and differentiating into a wide range of specialized cell types.

"*Conversations with God* says that the purpose of life is to recreate ourselves anew in the next grandest version of the greatest vision ever we held about Who We Are. *This is precisely what is going on in your body right now.*

"Medical science has now learned that stem cells can be "coaxed" into becoming cells of *any part of the body whatsoever* . . . including heart or brain cells!

"Now if God can create something as marvelous as undifferentiated cells in all multi-cellular organisms that can become any body part at all, what do you suppose God can do with *Itself*?"

The audience grew silent.

"Could we call God simply Undifferentiated Life, from which all Individuated Life emerges? Would it be so far-fetched to imagine God as the Mother of All Stem Cells?"

CHAPTER 22

The Mechanism of Manifestation

S o much for Part One of the Process of Personal Creation, what I have called the *I am*. God is the *formless form*. God is *life*, the fundamental and basic and essential energy, the first and only element, in *undifferentiated form*.

Now for Part Two: what I have called the *You Are*. This is the Unspoken Truth about the process; this is the truth *behind* the truth: You are a *differentiation* of the Undifferentiated Form that is God.

Let me repeat that, so that the awesome implication is not missed. *You are a differentiation of the Undifferentiated Form that is God.*

Some of what God is has differentiated as *us*, and some of the unlimited energy that God is remains undifferentiated—waiting for us to differentiate it!

Now things get a little complicated here so...yes, you know already . . . keep tracking.

As noted now several times, God has already differentiated Itself in the realm of No-Time in every form there ever was, is now, and ever will be. The work of life is done. Its mission has been accomplished. It has individuated into everything already. This means that everything in the Field of Infinite Possibilities is there *already*. Or, to put it another way, it is there, *all ready!*

All we have to do is call it forth, bringing it into our reality. This is Part Three of the Process of Personal Creation, the *How To* part! Book after book has been written on this, but none has seriously attempted to explain the *mechanism* by which manifestation works.

We know now that just as medical science can "coax" stem cells to take on the form of any cell in the body, creating heart tissue, bones, and even brain tissue to replace damaged body parts, so, too, can God "coax" Its Undifferentiated Form into any physical shape or non-physical form whatsoever—and has done so! These many shapes and forms are called *life!*

(An example of a "non-physical form" is a feeling. For instance, God can appear in a person's life in the form of love. Or a feeling of forgiveness. Or—as often happens at the moment of a person's death—a feeling of being totally safe and embraced and "welcomed home." Those feelings are *God*, in non-physical form.)

The *Mechanism of Manifestation* is a process that begins with "remembering" Who We Really Are (we are one of the many forms of this "shape-shifting God") and all that we have already done (we have created everything that is), and then remembering specific aspects of what has already been created.

When we separated our Selves from God in order to produce the experience of Individuation, we did so by dismembering our Divine Self from all of our creations.

Now, when we choose to make any aspect of Our Divine Self manifest in our reality, all we have to do is remember that creation. *We do this through the expressions of life called thoughts, words, actions, and feelings.*

How does this work? Well, it is really quite simple. Everything in life is energy. *Everything.* Everything in life is vibrating. *Everything.* Vibration is the movement of energy. It is The Essence, manifesting Itself in differing form through the elegant process of movement.

Everything is connected to everything else. *Everything.* There is *nothing* that is "disconnected" or "dismembered." We only *think* that there is. Disconnection and dismembering is impossible.

The All Of Everything really *is* an enormous, larger than fathomable *matrix.* The matrix is vibrating at differing frequencies in different locations. These differences could be called local disturbances in the energy field—like a pebble dropped into a pond.

You are a local disturbance. So are your thoughts, your words, your actions. Words vibrate. Thoughts vibrate. Actions vibrate. Words are nothing more than sounds, of course, and sound is nothing more than the vibration of energy at certain frequencies. Thoughts are less dense, and so vibrate at different frequencies. Actions are more dense, and vibrate at still other frequencies.

The act of "creation" is simply the act of tuning into the vibration of that which already exists in the All of Everything, which attunement draws it to you. You are not really "creating" anything, but merely noticing that it has already been created, and magnetizing it—or *attracting* it.

The process of *attraction* is simply a matter of adjusting your own energy to match the energy of that which you wish to experience. Again, you are not creating anything, you are merely experiencing the *already created*. You do this by pulling it to you, by "calling it forth" from the Field of Infinite Possibilities, through the "identicalizing" of your energies.

We have been told in *Conversations with God* that the three tools of creation are Thought, Word, and Action. Everything you think, everything you say, and everything you do creates energy—and thus, your reality. For your "reality" is *nothing more than the sum total of your energies and the energies they attract.*

The *Mechanism of Manifestation* is just "energy matching." It is the attuning of vibration to *resonate* with that aspect of universal energy which an Individuation desires to experience.

"Reality" is a word meaning "what is being experienced *right here, right now.*" Remember, that is the *only* thing that can be experienced. You cannot experience yesterday, you can only remember it. You cannot experience tomorrow, you can only antici-pate it. The *only thing in the Universe* that you can experience is Here and Now.

Nothing is really "real," it is only "real" to the degree that you are experiencing it. Another way to put this is that by experiencing it, you *make* it real.

Experiencing is all about resonating. It is about the energies of the Essence that you draw to you and through you right here, right now. You call this "creation."

Creation is resonation.

When you get an "idea" in your head about something, or "visualize" something (as inventors often do), all you are doing, in actuality, is remembering it as it already exists. If it did not already exist, *you could not think of it.*

"Thinking" is actually the act of *retrieving.* It is a process of reaching into the Eternal Collective Consciousness and retrieving data. It is the spontaneous resonation of a local Individuation of Divinity with an aspect of universal Divinity. It is a matching of a Part of Everything with the All of Everything.

That is why mental and intentional focus is so powerful and so vital to the creative (retrieval) process. By this process of intentional thinking and deep feeling, we do not DIScover so much as

REcover that for which we have been wishing. ("Even before you ask, I will have answered.")

This realization can often come to us abruptly, out of the blue. All at once we have "real-ized"—or *made real*—something that was always there.

I call this process of suddenly remembering, "spiritual recovery." It is very much like scientific discovery, only on a metaphysical level. Just as scientific discovery is the manifestation of something *already latent* in the order of nature, so, too, is spiritual recovery the manifestation of something *already latent* in the order of super-nature (or what some have called the supernatural—or, if you please . . . God).

An intellectual understanding of this process can help us to engage in the process itself. When we know what we are doing—and why—we are usually more adept at doing it.

The Essential Energy of Life could be described as wispy, ethereal, delicate. It is spread out everywhere, at once. The function of creation is to magnetize and magnify this energy, drawing it to you and making it larger in your experience.

Feeling is a powerful way to do this. It focuses energies into a resonating wave pattern. When you wish to manifest, seek not merely to think of a thing, but to feel it. *Feel* what it would be like to have that. *Feel* what it would be like to experience it. Feeling fine-tunes the morphic field that encases you and that you add to when you emit energy—which you do in every moment. Feeling is the way we identify and magnify the energy we wish to experience more of, by *resonating* with it.

As we become more and more aware of how the *Mechanism of Manifestation* works, we will find ourselves able to more easily manifest many things in our lives. Not only physical objects and experiences, but non-physical feelings and awareness.

Thus, we can manifest not only money, but the experience called Right Livelihood; not only a companion, but the experience called Love; not only a physical solution to a problem, but the experience called Wisdom. Thus, we can manifest forgiveness, compassion, understanding, joy, happiness . . . and peace.

Peace on earth, goodwill to humans everywhere.

At last.

CHAPTER 23

Why the Process of Creation Has Been Kept under Wraps

L et's be clear about why so many of those who believe in a God to whom they appeal are upset by the idea of a "power" that exists inside of everyone that allows us to create our own reality.

When we have to go to God (that is, a God who exists outside of us, separate from us, away from us) to get help in time of need or to produce something in our life that we earnestly desire, the presumption is that we have to obey the laws of God in order to receive an affirmative response. We have to be in *good standing* with God in order for God to bless us. We have to be good with God if we want God to be good with us. It is a *quid pro quo.*

We have been taught that God will not bless those who disobey Him or ignore Him or do not come to Him in the *right way*. Indeed, God will do more than simply fail to bless such people. God will condemn them to eternal damnation. He will cause them to burn in the everlasting fires of hell.

Yet if we have the power *within us* to create what we want, that means *we don't have to be good people in order to get it.* In short, we don't have to obey the Law of God if we can use the Energy of Attraction and Personal Creation. This takes the power out of the hands of those who would tell us what the Law of God IS.

The implications of that last sentence are enormous. And they *have* been throughout human history. Which is why, throughout human history, those who would tell us what the Law of God *is* have arrested those who would tell us that the Kingdom of Heaven is within—and have often killed them.

There is one point on which you can expect most of the world's religions to agree. They may not agree on everything, but I can assure you most will agree on *this:* The power to control your own reality, to be happier than God, to create riches, fame, love, and joy in your life (to say nothing of peace on earth), does *not* lie within you, and it is arrogant and spiritually dangerous for you to imagine that it does.

God controls your life according to His Will, and your job is to obey the Will of God, submit to the Will of God, do the bidding of God, and, if you want something for yourself, hope and beg and pray that it is God's Will that you receive it.

There is another threat here as well, as religion sees it. When we go to God for help, or ask Him to create what we earnestly desire, there is no guarantee that God will do it—even if we *are* obeying God's Law. Even good people, even wonderful people, have had their prayers go unanswered. And when they ask about this, when they fly to their priests and their rabbis and their ulamas and beg to know, *Why did God not grant my request? Have I not been a good and faithful servant?*, they are told: "Mysterious are the ways of the Lord. Yours is not to question, but to accept."

Yet Personal Creation is said to work *without fail.* God may say "no," but Personal Creation only says "yes." It always produces results. It's simply a matter of what you put your attention to, what you feel most strongly.

This is the great threat of Personal Creation—and why it has been kept under wraps.

As long as we think that God might say "no" to any of our requests, we will do whatever we think (or whatever we are told) that it takes *to get God to say "yes."* And this is where control is exerted by religion, for it is religion which tells us what we must do to get a "yes" from God!

Personal Creation, on the other hand, responds with a "yes" to *every* appeal—and every thought is an appeal, every word is an appeal, every action is an appeal.

If this process really works, then extraordinary creative power has been placed in our hands. Way too *much* creative power, some organized religions feel, for them to continue to be able to justify their dogmas, doctrines, decrees, and decisions.

Thus, if you try to "create" something *of your own free will* you may be accused of apostasy, an act of rebellion not unlike the act of Satan, for he, too (religionists tell us), proclaimed himself in his hubris to have the Power of God, to be equal to God, to be as glorious as God—and for this he was cast out of heaven and condemned to the everlasting torture of separation from the Divine, in the company of those wretched enough to be sent to Hades to join him.

The true danger of Personal Creation is that it involves thinking of yourself in a new way . . . and thinking of *God* in a new way.

These are the two unbelievable things that Jesus of Nazareth invited us to do, and he was crucified for it.

Think of yourself in a new way, he said, and think of God in a new way. He didn't say it in those words, but the words he used meant exactly the same thing. And he said other things, too, very directly revealing Great Truth.

The ideas that Jesus shared with the people of his time hit his world like a thunderbolt. He went around saying things such as, "Ask, and it shall be given you; seek, and ye shall find; knock, and it shall be opened unto you. For every one that asketh receiveth; and he that seeketh findeth; and to him that knocketh it shall be opened."

This is, of course, exactly what Personal Creation is about. It is exactly what teachers like Émile Coué and Rev. Dr. Norman Vincent Peale and Harold Sherman were trying to tell us many years ago. It is exactly what Esther and Jerry Hicks are saying today (and have been saying for many years), it is what Wayne Dyer shares with us, and what *Conversations with God* has articulated in such accessible and exciting ways, and what many teachers and messengers have been inviting us to embrace for hundreds of years.

It is true that not all of the messengers who have spoken of Personal Creation through the years have made it clear that what we are using is the power of God. But Jesus *was* clear. He said: "...what man is there among you whom, if his son ask for bread, will he give him a stone instead? Or if he ask for fish, will he give him a serpent? If even you, being evil, know how to give good gifts unto your children, how much more shall your Father which is in heaven give good things to them that ask him?"

So there is the missing link.

As has been noted, some people who hear about Personal Creation have criticized it, thinking that human beings are being encouraged to rely on themselves and to *exclude* God. In fact, master messengers are encouraging human beings to rely on themselves and to *include* God.

Yet these critics have a point, for many people have not been told something very important. They have not been told that . . .

The Energy of Attraction is one of the great Principles of Life, and that these principles are God's Process.

They have not been told that . . .

Using the Energy of Attraction is simply another way of using God.

When you understand this process and how it works, you have to *worry about nothing*. Jesus said this plainly. Shall we revisit his words?

"So don't go around asking, *'What are we to eat?'* or *'What shall we drink?'* or *'Wherewithal will we clothe ourselves?'* . . . Seek ye first the kingdom of God and all these things shall be added unto you."

Ah-ha!, religionists could exclaim, *there it is!* Jesus declared point blank that it was about *going to God*. So much for going to *yourself!* Jesus said, 'Seek ye first the kingdom of God!'"

You can imagine, then, how upsetting it could be to them when they find that Jesus also said, many times: "The kingdom of God is within you."

CHAPTER 24

The Best Way to
Achieve Personal Goals

W hile all spiritual masters through the ages have advised us not to worry about the self, I want to repeat that it is very okay to have personal goals in life.

I wish to also note that when we understand that the best and quickest way to achieve all of our goals and to live the life of which we have dreamed is to assist *others* in achieving their goals and living the life of which *they* have dreamed, we will have found the key to lasting happiness.

I promise you, I am not just making this up. This is not just my good idea. This has been the experience of so many people who have made a huge success of their lives. Read the quotations below. Just read them and absorb them. These words are from people who have reason to know How Life Works.

In helping others, we shall help ourselves, for whatever good we give out completes the circle and comes back to us.
—Flora Edwards

Our prime purpose in this life is to help others.
—Dalai Lama

Help others achieve their dreams and you will achieve yours.
—Les Brown

*It is literally true that you can succeed best
and quickest by helping others to succeed.*
—Napoleon Hill

*You can have anything in the world you want if you'll
just help enough other people get what they want.*
—Zig Ziglar

I find it intriguing that so many highly successful people have come up with the same formula, the same understanding, the same insight, the same approach, the same basic description of a way of living that was given to us so long ago . . .

Do unto others as you would have it done unto you.

When we see others as Divine and *treat* others as Divine, the Energy of Attraction will be used, at last, as it was designed to be used: to bring *to* us the reality *of* us.

And not just to some of us, but to all of us; not just to a few of us, but to every last one of us.

CHAPTER 25

The Process of Personal Creation and the Pain in the World

By now you may wondering about those 17 Steps to Greater Happiness, and I want you to know that we will be getting to them shortly. But before we get too deeply into how you, personally, can be *happier than God*, we must look at a matter that we brushed past at the very outset of this book, but that I promised we would explore and explain before we said goodbye.

What of the people who are suffering, who are in pain, who are oppressed and living in misery?

For most "positive thinkers" and proponents of Personal Creation there appears to be no answer for the kind of stinging criticism that I reprinted earlier.

To refresh your memory . . .

By far the most offensive part of the message is the suggestion that people who have pain in their lives are somehow attracting it with their thoughts. Darfur rape victims did not ask for it. Children who are molested did not ask for it. Starving Africans did not ask for it.

*To suggest that their "incorrect thinking" is the
cause of this is sickening . . .*

If "incorrect thinking" is *not* the cause of all this
suffering, then what is? Fate?

The answer is, of course, that it *is* humanity's
manner of thinking that is the root cause of humanity's great suffering, yet it is not as simple as saying
that. For it is not merely the thinking of those who
are suffering. It is the thinking of everyone.

———

It is true that many of those who are suffering—
who are living in constant turmoil or abject
poverty—have taken to considering the present situation their "lot in life." They have given in, given up.
They have rejected peaceful, non-violent rebellion as
pointless or impossible, and by their silent consent
they have unwittingly—certainly not purposefully—
extended the conditions they inherited from those in
their culture or society who have gone before them.

And so to some degree it *is* the thinking of
those who are suffering, it is their continuing subconscious or unconscious thought, that plays a role
in creating the realities they endure. Of course, they
did not ask for such conditions and experiences.

That is not what is being said here. Yet to deny that the ongoing, continual state of mind of many people within a culture has nothing to do with the experience of that culture is to deny the evidence right before us.

But now it should be noted—indeed, it *must* be noted—that to a huge extent the suffering of entire cultures and peoples is also created by the collective consciousness of those elsewhere who *are not* suffering. For it is many of those who are not suffering who allow the suffering of others to continue, turning a deaf ear to pleas for help, and often saying that at some level it is their own fault, or surely, at least, their own responsibility.

This "let them eat cake" consciousness, together with the hopelessness of those who *are* suffering, creates a virtual *wall of thought* that it would be difficult for any group or individual to get over, get past, or get around.

It must be understood that Personal Creation works collectively as well as individually, and that is what is being discussed here. There is such a thing as *collective consciousness*, and it is very powerful. The combined thoughts of the many do play their effect on the combined experience of the few.

In fact, "fate" *is* the reason that masses of people suffer while other groups of people do not, if we consider "fate" to be an acronym for: From All Thoughts Everywhere.

"Fate" is created by the sum total of everyone's ideas about a thing. It is very difficult (although not entirely impossible) for an individual in any closed group or society to overcome the sum total of everyone's ideas *within* that society, to say nothing about those outside of it.

Some individuals have overcome this huge energy obstacle and have risen, against all odds, to tremendous heights within societies or groupings where most others have not. We often call these individuals "heroes" and we erect statues to them and name buildings and bridges after them and put their picture on our money. While others have suffered, they have succeeded. Yet what makes the difference? How can this happen?

The answer, inevitably, has to do with how that those individuals were thinking. It has to do with how they "held" their idea of themselves vis-à-vis the whole. It has to do with how they were able to *overcome* the consciousness around them, and, indeed, the collective consciousness of huge swaths of humanity, which was working against them. It had to do with their using the power of individual determination, commitment, and their innermost ideas of Who They Are in relation to everything and everyone around them.

There is, really, very little question about this. When you talk with such people this is exactly what most of them will tell you. This is what they say to graduating classes at high schools and colleges, where they are inevitably asked to deliver commencement addresses. Everyone wants to know *how did they do it?* What is their *secret of success?*

Very few of them, the tiniest percentage of them, will tell you, "Oh, I did nothing. I had nothing to do with it. It was a lucky break." Most of them will say to those graduating classes, "Make no mistake about this. You make your own luck."

Does this apply to the starving children of Africa? To the raped women of Darfur?

No. Of course not. Not in the specific sense. People are not making their own luck by sitting down and imagining themselves in such situations, or by consciously using "incorrect thinking" and thus placing themselves there.

It is true that, as mentioned above, some people, in all societies and cultures, fear certain things and unconsciously dwell on those fears to such a degree that they do draw to themselves something of the things they fear. And, yes, a culture of suffering *can* develop. But that is not what others are talking about when they say that they are sickened by the suggestion that people bring on their own troubles by "incorrect thinking."

This statement rings hollow in my heart as well. Yet I know that what can and does happen is that the powerful energy of collective consciousness—which is perhaps the most powerful creative force of all—places in *all* our lives unhappy experiences and tragic outcomes . . . outcomes to which individuals fall prey even though they obviously do not consciously choose to.

Can collective consciousness, then, overcome individual conscious choice? Yes. Does it have to remain that way for every individual? No.

Jesus himself cried out in a loud voice, *Eli, Eli, lama sabachthani?* And few people remember that he was uttering, in the time of his own suffering, words from the Old Testament, which he, of course, knew well...

"My God, my God, why hast Thou forsaken me?" (Psalm 22:1-3).

It is precisely because massive collective consciousness can overcome individual consciousness and individual awareness that collective consciousness is so important—and why raising the collective consciousness of humanity is so vital.

The way to raise the collective consciousness of humanity is, of course, to raise the *individual* consciousness of human beings. Which is why telling people about Personal Creation is good, not bad; affirmative, not negative; something to be encouraged, not something to be put down and ridiculed and "made wrong" because someone isn't getting all the words exactly right.

So we know that even spiritual masters of the highest order can find themselves at the effect of mass consciousness. We see, then, that surely the suffering people of Darfur and the starving in Africa and molested children and others in our world who are deeply injured, individually and collectively, are certainly not at "fault" in the matter.

Yet the question is not whether they are "at fault." (No one teaching about Personal Creation or the Energy of Attraction, by the way, has ever suggested such a thing. This is a straw man, a manufactured conclusion drawn by those who would unfairly characterize their message.) The question is whether the Divine Gift of Personal Creation given to all human beings can be used to alleviate such suffering.

And the answer, of course, is yes.

Jesus stands as one breathtaking example of this. It is clear that Jesus was not the victim of his circumstances, but the Creator of them. His call to God was a moment of forgetfulness. I am so very glad that it was recorded in the Bible, because it signals to all of us that even the greatest of masters can have a moment of forgetfulness, and gives us great hope when we, too, experience such weak memories, imagining ourselves to be the victim of our circumstance, rather than to be at cause in the matter.

Yet Jesus rose to his own higher understanding in the next moment, using Personal Creation to continue on his journey, and we can, too. That, too, was his example for us to follow. And there have been others as well throughout human history who have been such examples for us, even in the time of their greatest travail. Nelson Mandela comes to mind contemporarily.

(I am sure that Mr. Mandela may feel uncomfortable being mentioned in the same context as Jesus, yet was not his response to his oppressors a

Christ-like response? And has he not set an example not only for his own people, but for the world entire?)

Yet now, a question. If all human beings can act in this way, even in the midst of their forgetfulness, why do we not do so? Do we see ourselves as victims of our own impotence? Do we imagine that our lives and our world are showing up the way they are because this is, at some level, what God wants?

If so, we are badly and sadly mistaken. The world is the way it is today not because God wants it that way, but because we do.

We do.

If we did not, we could change the world overnight. We could eliminate the pain and the damage and the sadness and the suffering in the blink of an eye. We could put an end to oppression and repression and depression so fast it would make your head spin. We could eliminate poverty and starvation and hopelessness in one fell swoop.

We could do all of this if we wanted to; if we really wanted to. The truth is, we do not want to. Individually, we may (in some cases). Collectively, we clearly do not, *or it would be done.*

Nothing that has been inflicted upon humanity by humanity is impossible for humanity to reverse. I encourage all of us to remember that always, and to carry that as the banner of a compassionate and caring people.

Nothing that has been inflicted on Humanity by Humanity is impossible for Humanity to reverse.

I believe that we will one day reverse the conditions of poverty and oppression and powerlessness and all the human-caused suffering of our species. And I believe that day will be coming sooner rather than later. I believe human beings everywhere are soon going to rise up and demand it, out of a new sense of who we are and how we want life to be on this planet. And I believe that many individuals will lead the way in this spiritual revolution by demonstrating that it is possible to *be happier than God.*

I'll go further. I think that people like you—*you*, reading this book right now—would be willing to help in beginning this process if you thought there was a way to do that.

Well, there is.

CHAPTER 26

How to Use the Process of Personal
Creation to Help the Whole World

Chapter 20

How to Use the Plan, and to Broadcast
it to the Whole World

The purpose of life and the purpose of Personal Creation *is the same*. This is not something that most people put together in their head, and it is definitely not something that enough teachers of the Energy of Attraction are making clear.

The purpose of life and of Personal Creation is to bring you—and *every human being on the earth*—the grandest experience of who you are, to cause you to be happier than God, thus to advance the evolution of the soul. Both the individual soul and the One Soul That Is.

This is a soul journey we are on, having nothing to do with the human body. It has no more to do with your body than a bookcase that you built has to do with the hammer and saw you used to build it. Like the hammer and saw, your body is simply your tool. Nothing else. Simply that.

You can use that tool to gratify your own personal whims or to help the whole world. That choice is yours.

If you think you are your body, you may be tempted to make the first choice. If you believe that your body is something you *have*, not something you *are*, you may be inspired to make the second choice.

It is therefore important to always remember who you are. Say three times each day, morning, noon, and night: "I am not my body. My body is what I have, it is not what I am."

This will help you to stay focused on your real identity, your real purpose for being here, your real reason for living, and the purpose of Personal Creation itself.

It is true that this process can be used to bring you every wonderful thing in life, anything at all that you desire. It is also true that you define yourself by what you say you desire. And it is *also* true that the process works best, and fastest, when you desire for others what you wish to experience for yourself. As explained earlier, this is because of *The Multiplier Effect.*

We are working with energy here. When all is said and done we must realize that we are simply working with raw energy. Thoughts are energy. Things are energy. Emotions and feelings and experiences are energy. *God* is energy. *Life* is energy expressed.

Everything is energy.

When you want for the whole world what you want for yourself—peace, joy, wisdom, happiness, and love—you multiply the energy you send out.

When you do this at the same time that many others are doing it, you *multiply your multiplication*. You have increased your Impact Potential exponentially. You have literally harnessed the power of God. ("Wherever two or more are gathered, there am I.")

This is important, because with regard to the challenges facing the world, the axiom is:

The energy that creates the solution must be equal to the energy that creates the problem.

Albert Einstein observed that you cannot solve a problem using the same energy that created it. That is true. It must be a different kind of energy, but it must be of *the same intensity*.

Whether you call the tools that you use to create this energy intensity prayer, meditation, positive thinking, Personal Creation, the *Mechanism of Manifestation*, the "formula," the "mystery," or the "secret," they are all the same thing. They are all part of a process than can bring us to greater happiness. They are all a functioning of, a putting to intentional use of, the process of *life itself*, the way of the universe. This is God's process. This is the way God moves.

Émile Coué called this process "optimistic autosuggestion." The application of his familiar conscious autosuggestion, "Every day, in every way, I'm getting better and better" (*Tous les jours à tous points de vue je vais de mieux en mieux*), is the best known example of what is often called Couéism or the Coué method, according to the writers of Wikipedia, who also tell us: It was in 1913 that Coué founded the Lorraine Society of Applied Psychology. His book *Self Mastery Through Conscious Autosuggestion* caused a sensation on its publication in England in 1920 and in the United States two years later.

Such "revelations" have *always* caused a sensation—just as the revealing of "the secret" is causing today. Yet always the sensation tends to die down, and the world returns to its Old Ways.

Historically humanity has sparked itself with a glimmer of hope, then returned to its sadness and its anguish, its turmoil and its conflict, its pain and its suffering. For the forces mounted against New Revelations have throughout the ages (and yes, even in this "enlightened" time) beaten back the message of inner personal empowerment in favor of an edict of continuing reliance on sources exterior—namely, religion, government, and Those In Charge.

That's been the history, but all that can change if we will but place *ourselves* in the category of Those in Charge.

Will humanity do it?

I believe the answer is yes, and that it will happen when People Power and God Power are reconciled; when one is not made to devalue or dishonor the other.

Many people ask me, "What can I do to help change the world? What can one person do?"

There is a great deal that one person can do. And the first thing that any person can do is *leverage* individual intent, expanding it to *globally impacting proportion*. This is done by the simple use of *The Multiplier Effect.*

Here are some suggestions on how you can use Personal Creation and *The Multiplier Effect* to create joy and happiness, peace, and prosperity for all the world:

- Start a Focusing Creation For All The World group. Meet once a week by telephone (this group can be worldwide!) and spend three minutes focusing your combined attention, with clear intention, on a particular outcome you wish to see in the world. This is the wonderful and powerful tool of Focusing Creation for others, rather than simply for the self. It uses the Multiplier Effect, and can produce startling results surprisingly fast.

- Remember that collective attention *with clear intention* is the key. Do not just think about a problem in the world. Think about *the outcome that you intend to produce.* I call this Intention Attention. I can tell you from personal experience that it is extremely effective.

• Do not make the outcome you wish to produce too generic, such as "world peace" or "greater prosperity for all people." Rather, call forth a particular outcome. Say words with your thoughts that describe specific experiences. *See* these outcomes. Run scenes of them, like a film, on the movie screen of your mind. Invite your group to do so, too. An interesting experiment might be to actually *draw* pictures of the future. These can be simple images, cartoon figures. You don't have to be a master artist to place on paper the visions you wish to manifest into reality. Another technique is to create a Vision Board, with actual photographs, cut out of newspapers or magazines or wherever you can find them, of the outcomes you wish to manifest. Cut out a picture of a family feast, and beneath it write: *The world's starving people.* These and other techniques can and do work. They are all simply tools with which to sharply focus your thoughts and to arouse your feelings, which means your spiritual energy.

- Do not change the outcome that you wish to call forth from week to week, but continue focusing on a single outcome for at least several sessions.

- If you wish to increase the power of the energy focus during a particular period of acute crisis in the world, you may choose to hold your Focusing Creation calls more than once a week. As sponsor of the call, you may schedule them whenever you wish. Those who can join you will do so. Those who cannot will be on the next call. Trust that.

- Hold a Focusing Creation class or study group in your own home twice a month. Share with others the information you now have about *all three parts* of the "secret" (Part Three, *How To*, is wonderfully described in the extraordinary book by Esther and Jerry Hicks, *The Law of Attraction: The Basic Teachings of Abraham*, which you may wish to use as a teaching text. You may also wish to obtain and show the movie *The Secret*.

Then, expand to other texts that also discuss this wonderful tool, including the one you are holding in your hand, and the other titles I have mentioned in this text.)

- Join a global community choosing to use the Energy of Attraction for purposes larger than personal enrichment and satisfaction of personal desires. (A note about one way you may do that appears at the end of this book.)

- Subscribe to the Creating For All The World monthly E-News (at www.nealedonaldwalsch.com) *and contribute to its content.* Tell the world of *your* experiences with Personal Creation, both for yourself and for your world, and invite others across the globe to join in this Focusing Creation process, so that everyone may be *so happy they can't stand it*, experiencing the wonder and the joy and the happiness of communion with God through Personal Creation.

• Listen to the monthly Focusing Creation teleconference (information about which may be found at www.nealedonaldwalsch.com), where people around the world join together to hear a new "lecturette" each month and then ask questions and share their experiences of bringing peace and harmony, joy and abundance, fulfillment, and the miracle of self-realization to the people of the world and to their own lives!

These are just a few of the things you can do to enlarge the scope and expand the horizon of your work with Personal Creation, thereby rendering "attraction" the greatest tool the world has ever known for creating Peace on Earth and joy in the collective heart of humanity.

And finally, *don't leave yourself out*. Remember what was said here. It is totally okay for you to include yourself in the list of people around the world for whom you wish to call forth peace, prosperity, and love. Allow yourself to use the Energy of Attraction to call forth all the joy and wonder that life can bring you, in whatever form you happily choose!

CHAPTER 27

17 Steps to Being
Happier than God

Okay, we've created a deep contextual field within which to consider the steps I outlined at the beginning of our explorations here. Now let's look at these powerful steps that you might take to make your life more joyful, more peaceful, more fulfilling, more exciting, more rewarding, and more *fun*.

I believe that the whole of humanity can be *happier than God*. This will occur following the second great reformation of humanity's religions.

Don't be discouraged. That is on its way. Sooner rather than later, it is going to happen. I was told in the dialogue called *Tomorrow's God* that it would take place within 25 to 30 years—or less, depending on world conditions.

The world is losing patience with itself. Its people can see that the way we are proceeding, the way we are co-creating life on the earth, is not sustainable. They also see that it is many (but certainly not all) of our most fundamental beliefs about God and about life that are causing our dysfunctional behaviors. So you can look for a major shift in our religious experience, with it transforming itself into what I have been calling the New Spirituality, in the not very distant future.

In the meantime, you can be enormously happier on a personal level than you have ever been before—no matter *how* happy you have been!

Here are 17 Steps that can get you there.

1. Bring an end to Separation Theology.

Work in your own life and your personal belief system to eliminate any thought of separation from God. Just get rid of that theology.

Separation Theology is a theology that insists that we are "over here" and God is "over there." Its doctrine tells us that God separated us from God as punishment for our sins, and that our job now is to get back to God, which is possible only if God will allow it, which God will do only if we obey God's commands, follow God's laws, and submit to God's will. In short, we must do What God Wants. (For my separate exploration of this subject, see *What God Wants*, from Atria Books, 2006.)

This Separation Theology has produced a Separation Cosmology (that is, a way of looking at all of life on this planet that includes *separation* as its basic principle), which, in turn, has produced a Separation Sociology (that is, a way of socializing our species that requires us to act as separate beings serving our own best and separate interests), which has produced a Separation Pathology (that is, *pathological behavior* producing suffering, conflict, violence, and death by our own hands).

Only when our Separation Theology is replaced by a Unity Theology will our Separation Pathology be healed. We must come to understand that all of life is One. This is your first step and it is mine. It is the jumping off point. It is the beginning of the end of how things now are. It is the start of a new creation, of the placing into reality of the next grandest version of the greatest vision ever you held about who you are.

The Unspoken Truth reveals to us that Oneness is not a characteristic of life . . . life is a characteristic of Oneness.

Life is the *expression* of Oneness Itself. *God* is the expression of Oneness Itself. Life and God are One. Oneness is God and life. It is a circle.

When we understand this, we see God in everyone and in everything. Including our divine selves.

We see clearly that we are God *Godding.* That is, God in the act of recreating Godself. God, and life, *evolves.* God never stays the same, but becomes bigger and more of what God *is*, in every moment.

God is more of everything now than God was a nanosecond ago. When we solve our own case of "mistaken identity," when we identify ourselves as That Which God Is, we will be as happy as God.

But now follow this: If we use the term "God" to indicate the Collective Divinity and the term "you" to indicate the Individuation of Divinity, and if the day comes when you have raised your consciousness to a level where you are happier than many other Individuations . . . well, then, you will be *happier than "God."*

The Individuation that is "You" will be of higher consciousness than the largest number of other individuations of Divinity that we call "God," just as previous messengers and avatars and masters (Buddha, Moses, Jesus, Muhammad, and more) have experienced *their* Individuated Consciousness to be raised above the level of the Collective Consciousness. It then became their mission to *raise the Collective Consciousness* of humanity so that the *Entirety Which Is God* could evolve even further, continuing to expand in consciousness and total self-awareness.

This is what they were doing here.

All of life is Divine, and when we treat all of life *as* Divine we will change everything. For how can one aspect, how can a single Individuation of Divinity, ever be totally happy so long as any other Individuation is totally unhappy? The answer is, it cannot. And so, we will raise each other up, that we might *all* experience ourselves, one by one, being "happier than God."

"I am come that you may have life, and have it more abundantly," said one Master. And the Master-in-You will one day say the same thing. When the earth is thus transformed, person by person, no more will children die of starvation. No more will millions suffer from oppression. No more will nation battle nation. When we treat everyone as Divine, there will be war no more.

2. *Stay in touch with who you are.*

Remember that you are not your body, but a soul traveling with the body on a journey to joy. Remember that your soul is an everlasting part of God. Remember that you and God are One. Then become clear on what is most important to that Individuation of Divinity that is manifesting as You, right here, right now. Treat everything and everyone as if it was perfectly tuned to everything and perfectly timed to your soul's agenda. Understand that because of Who You Are, nothing can hurt you, and there is nothing you need to be absolutely happy in this when/where of your eternal existence.

What I am saying here is to see yourself as a Spiritual Being with a body, on the sacred mission of self-realization and self-creation. First, realize Who You Really Are, then re-create yourself anew in the next grandest version of the greatest vision you ever held about that. Your task each day—and it is not as difficult as it may at first seem—is this: Remember your identity. Retain your identity. Recreate your identity.

Remember your identity in the face of every evidence to the contrary.

Retain your identity in the face of every situation that would deny it.

Recreate your identity in the face every invitation from life to stay right where you are.

3. Give others every experience you seek.

The fastest and easiest way to retain your identity is to place others in touch with theirs. The fastest way to have *any* experience is to cause others to have the same experience. If you wish to experience your Divine Self and your true identity, cause another to experience their Divine Self and their true identity.

Give people back to themselves.

You can do this in a hundred ways in a thousand lives in a million moments.

Whatever you wish to experience in your own lifetime, cause another to experience in theirs. If you wish to experience love, cause another to be loved. If you wish to experience abundance, cause another to be abundant. If you wish to experience success, cause another to be successful. If you wish to experience power, cause another to be powerful. If you wish to experience wisdom, cause another to be wise. If you wish to experience romance, cause another to be romanced. If you wish to experience forgiveness, cause another to be forgiven. If you wish to experience safety and security, cause another to be safe and secure. If you wish to experience perfect partnership, cause another to be perfectly partnered. If you wish to experience peace, cause another to be at peace.

What I am saying here is that Personal Creation begins best with another. Focus first on the other, the other, always the other, never first on the Self, and that which the Self wishes to experience will be realized sevenfold. Whatever you wish to create for yourself, create for another. This is the Energy of Attraction at its most powerful.

Why this works: What you bring to another, you bring to the Self, for there is no other in ultimate reality. There is only the Self. When you understand this, you understand everything you will ever need to know about how to be happier than God.

4. Be clear that nothing you see is real.

We live in the world of illusion. (See *Communion with God* for an extraordinary discussion of the Ten Illusions of Humans.) You will understand your true relationship with everything around you when you think of yourself as a magician observing his own tricks. Have the fun that a good magician has, but don't forget for a moment that it is all an illusion. More important, don't forget that it is you who are *creating* the illusion. Endeavor, therefore, not to get lost in it.

What I am saying here is to stay above the fray by noticing that are you creating your experience of all of it. Exterior circumstances may present themselves in a wide variety of ways, but the way that you respond and

react to them is entirely under your control. The
moment that you choose your response, and do so freely
and in full awareness, is the moment that you recreate
yourself anew. This is the Power Moment. This is the
Time of Magic. This is the Intentioned Instant, in
which what you choose to become reveals itself in your
experienced reality. This is when you decide about
yourself, and see yourself being what you have decided
to be, sequentaneously. (This is the experience of a
thing occurring both sequentially and simultaneously.)

Know always that what is happening is what is
happening, but how you are experiencing what is hap-
pening is something you are making up.

5. Decide that you are not your "story."

In order to experience what is happening in a
way that preserves your happiness you will most
likely have to drop your story.

Your "story" is all the data that you have col-
lected about what has happened to you in your life,
and the reality that you have manufactured about the
kind of person you and other people are and how
you all got to be that way.

For instance, I was dunked under water when I
was a child of about eight. I did not know how to

swim yet, so I was floating and playing around in an inner tube when some big bullies just decided to tip me over in water that was way above my head. They didn't know that I couldn't swim, but *I knew it* and I never forgot the ice-cold fear that quickly turned to heart-thumping panic as I flailed about, trying to get air into my lungs. For many years, until well into my adulthood, I did not go near the water. At least, no further than where my feet could touch bottom.

All of us have stories such as this, and all of us have a million of them. Our stories are made up of incidents large and small, spread out across a lifetime. We become the sum total of these encounters—unless we do not. At some point we may let go of an idea that we hold about ourselves and others, because we realize we have to if we wish to get on with life.

Happiness will never be found in your story, only in your newest and grandest decision about yourself and others. This may mean having to tell yourself, with regard to a lot of things that have occurred, "That was 'then' and this is 'now.'" None of those things have any bearing on what is occurring in this moment.

A boy has been raised by an overbearing, demanding, critical mother for whom nothing was ever quite good enough. He leaves his mother's home at 18 and gets on with his life, to which he seems to have adjusted fairly well. At 23 he falls in love and marries. A few months later his wife encounters a behavior of his that she finds a touch annoying. (It might be nothing big. It could be something very small, actually. He never puts the cap back on the toothpaste...) She mentions it to him, and he blows up. "Hey! Get off my back! Just . . . get-off-my-back." She looks at him, stunned. Where is this coming from?

It is coming from his reactive mind. Yet the invitation of transformation is for you to come from your creative mind. It is to create yourself brand new, the way you would like to be, not the way you have always been. Even though you have good reasons for being the way you have always been.

It is important to understand that your subconscious mind does not know the difference between Then and Now. It holds all data in a place where time does not exist. That is why you can break out in a cold sweat dreaming about something that occurred 20 years ago. Your subconscious mind (which controls most of your body's systems, by the way) does not know that what you are remembering is not actually happening.

To react is to do exactly what the word suggests. It is to "act again, as you did before." This is a sure path to unhappiness, for the greatest happiness is creation, not reaction.

What I am saying here is that what life is inviting you to do is to experience yourself, and the moment you are living in any given when/where, in the way that you wish to experience yourself, rather than the way that you used to experience yourself.

You are invited to give up your previous identity, let go of your prior idea about yourself, and pretend that life has started all over for you right now, at least with regard to the most important decisions regarding who you are and how it is with you. In some circles this is called being born again.

6. Have only preferences.

Many people make themselves unhappy simply by finding it impossible to accept life just as it is presenting itself right here, right now. Nothing is ever good enough, not is ever quite right. Like the Princess and the Pea, there is no way these people can ever get comfortable with their situation or circumstance, their surroundings or the company they keep. Nothing works, nothing is good enough, fast enough, big enough. As long as there is a thing called "weather" these folks can find some reason to not be totally happy. They cannot celebrate what *is*, but need, rather, to excoriate what is *not*.

To celebrate or excoriate, that is the choice in every moment. Choose the first and not the second, and your life can be filled with smiles forever. You see, there *is* a way to be happier than God, and that is to not require anything to be any different at all from the way it is right now.

This does not mean never to seek to change anything. It *does* mean not to base your happiness on whether or not that change occurs. This is about shifting from addictions to preferences in the living of your life.

If you are offered a bowl of vanilla ice cream and the truth is that you prefer chocolate, it is perfectly okay (and very healthy, in fact) to indicate your preference. ("Thank you so much, you are very kind. But may I ask, might there be any chocolate ice cream in the house? To be honest, that's my absolute favorite!")

The result of this kind of honest exchange could be that you wind up with your favorite! And the worst that can happen is that you wind up with vanilla, which is okay, too, because your taste for chocolate is a preference, not an addiction.

You can always tell whether you are addicted to something, as opposed to merely preferring something, by looking to see if the absence of it causes you to abandon your happiness.

In the example above, the presumption is that you would not be unhappy if you did not get chocolate ice cream, but that you would be perfectly happy with vanilla. Chocolate, then, is merely a preference, not an addiction.

The idea in life is to change your addictions into preferences. I was first introduced to this concept in the extraordinary *Handbook to Higher Consciousness* by Ken Keyes Jr. I recommend this deeply insightful book to everyone.

Transforming addictions to preferences is done by the simple expedient of taking an honest look at how much you would really be missing if you did not get what you think you want and need right here, right now. Often, it is very much less than you might have thought.

What I'm saying here is that there is always something to celebrate, so long as life is being lived. Seeing your cup as half full rather than half empty is more than a sappy aphorism. It is the key to enduring happiness.

If you will step out of your story long enough to take an honest look, and to give life a fair chance, you will notice that in almost every instance life is showing up right now *with everything you need to be content and at peace. All you have to do to experience this is to change your requirement of this present moment.*

Requirement changing is really very easy. It is simply a matter of changing your mind about what you need this instant. The truth is that you need nothing in particular. "Need" is one of the Ten Illusions of Humans. It is not real. It may be challenging for you to embrace this idea as part of your living reality, but it may not be so much of a stretch to see that surely most of the things that you felt you could never live without were not required at all. You've found a way not only to exist, but to smile, laugh, and be happy without them.

"Requirement" is another of the Ten Illusions of Humans. (For the complete list, and an explanation of it, see the addendum.) This is the illusion that suggests that there is something that you absolutely, positively must have in order to live. Yet there is nothing that you must have other than what you have right now, which is the Self as it really is. You cannot die and your life cannot end, because you are life itself, made manifest. When you understand this you no longer fear death, and then you know longer fear life. Nor do you ever again feel an urgent, stomach-churning need for anything in particular. This changes everything.

219

7. See the perfection.

See everything for what it is: the perfect event perfectly timed to provide you with the perfect opportunity to express in the perfect way that which is Perfection Itself. As it relates to you, personally, perfection is the Self that you have chosen to be, and are now choosing to demonstrate and experience.

This is something that most people cannot admit and refuse to acknowledge, yet it is the truth about you—and God knows it. What I have learned as a result of my direct interactions with God is that I am Whole, Complete, and Perfect just the way I am. And so are you.

This applies to the saint and the sinner, the angel and the scoundrel. There are no sinners or scoundrels in God's world. There are only Individuations of Divinity, some of whom have forgotten Who They Really Are.

Our opportunity in each golden moment of Now is to *use* that moment, and all that it holds and offers, to *remember* Who We Really Are—and then to demonstrate that. Life gives us the gifts of eternity and infinity so that we might know ourselves in our own experience . . . and then recreate ourselves anew in the next grandest version of the greatest vision ever we held about Who We Are.

This is the process we call *evolution*. This is God *godding*.

What I am saying here is to judge not, and neither condemn, the people and events being placed before you by life, but rest well in the awareness that you, yourself, have drawn them to you, that you might fulfill life's potential, its promise, and its purpose.

William Shakespeare wrote, "Nothing is evil lest thinking make it so." He was telling us that a thing is what you call it. With this insight he gave us the keys to the kingdom.

8. Bypass the drama.

Remember that nothing has any meaning save the meaning you give it. Repeat this quietly in your mind at any moment of stress or upset: *Nothing has any meaning save the meaning I give it.*

This is a variation on the words of Shakespeare, and I first heard it put this way in *A Course in Miracles*. These ten words can change your entire experience of life. They can stop drama in its tracks. They can cut turmoil and emotional distress in half. Indeed, they can eliminate them altogether.

Memorize these ten words and let them be your mantra when your day seems to be falling apart—or your career, or your relationship, or anything else that you have so carefully crafted and put into place. Remember that very often when life seems to be falling apart, it may actually be falling together for the first time.

When as a child I would become upset about things, my mother used to say to me, "How important do you think this will be when you're 90?" That would slow me down a bit, stopping me from "spinning out" into emotional self-indulgences that did no one (least of all me) any good.

"If you think you'll be sitting in your rocking chair on the front porch at 90 worried about this, then worry about it now. If you think you'll be upset about this then, be upset about it now. Otherwise, just let it go." That's what Mom would say.

I love those words. Let . . . it . . . go.

Let . . .

It . . .

Go . . .

Just breathe, and relax.

What I am saying here is to not jump into "reaction" mode at the first appearance of negative energy. Work hard with yourself to stay in the space of "creation." Realize that what you are seeing may be nothing more than the Law of Opposites playing its effect in the Process of Personal Creation. Go to a place of grat-

NEALE DONALD WALSCH

itude as often as you can . . . and don't be afraid to use humor as a way to get there. Self-deprecating humor, I have found, is just the ticket. It is just, absolutely, the very best. All I have to do to tamp down upset and unneeded drama in my life is to laugh at myself. It's great medicine.

9. Understand sadness.

There is a difference between sadness and unhappiness. During the writing of this book my dog, Lady, died. She had been my companion for over 14 years. In the past 12 months she had become increasingly pain-filled, from a variety of ailments and conditions. Toward the end she was stone deaf and could hardly walk. In the very last days she could not even raise herself up.

I was sad when she died, but I was not unhappy.

Can you see the difference?

This is *not an unimportant difference.* This is *not a trivial distinction.*

I was sad that Lady was no longer with me, but I was happy that she was no longer in pain. I was happy—very happy—that she had gone on with her journey, celebrating her Continuation Day.

I was even "happy that I was sad," because my sadness said something *to* me *about* me. It said that I cared. It said that I loved. It said that I was human, and that despite the way that the world was showing up around me, desensitizing everyone, I had stayed in touch with my humanity.

Yes, I was *happy* about my sadness, and about what it told me about Who I Am. It felt good to be sad.

Your sadness does not have to make you unhappy. Used as a marker of where you are on your evolutionary path, your sadness can be a source of inner confirmation of the depth of your feelings, and thus, of who you are as a person and a spiritual being.

Therefore, when someone dies, let yourself grieve. When someone hurts you, allow yourself sadness. And especially when you hurt someone else, allow sadness to accompany your regret. Give yourself the gift of sadness and you will find that you heal more quickly from every experience that would tempt you to forget your full identity.

What I am saying here is that your sadness about anything need not stop you from being happier than God—happier than you once were. Happiness is a cumulative thing. It becomes greater the more you feel it. I feel happier now than I did in the days before Lady

*laid down her body for the last time. I feel happier now
than when I was 50, happier than when I was 30, happier, in fact, that I have ever been before in my life.*

*And I have learned how to accommodate my sad-
ness and hold it* within *my happiness, making it a wonderful part thereof. Indeed, I have learned that
"happiness" is achieved through the simple process of
embracing all of* life *exactly as it is.*

10. Stop arguing with life.

So much of the lack of happiness that we feel in
our lives emerges from our judgments. We tend to
judge everything. The people around us, the circumstances they present, the events of the moment, and,
of course, ourselves.

Some folks don't miss a single opportunity to
get into their place of judgment. It's almost as if *life
itself* is on trial. Constantly.

What is especially interesting about most
human judgment is that people do not even use an
objective measure with which to make their determi-
nations. They mostly use a previous experience,
their own ideas, their own "story" as a basis upon
which to decide about another.

It never occurs to them, of course, that it could possibly be *their* experience, *their* ideas, *their* "story" that might be a bit askew. I've watched this from a distance enough to conclude that I am probably doing it, too. So I have made a real effort to move into self-reflection as a replacement for judgment of others.

When I am tempted to be judgmental, I look inside to see when it was that *I* acted that way in *my* life, where it was that *I* produced such outcomes in *my* life, how it was possible that *I* made such mistakes in *my* life. Suddenly, compassion rushes in, pushing judgment aside—and making condemnation impossible.

What I am saying here is that judgment has no place in a loving heart. Yet remember, judgment is not discernment, and observation is not judgment. It is perfectly healthy to be discerning, and it is perfectly natural to make observations. An "observation" says "what's so." A judgment says "so what?"

Least of all, judge yourself. For God will not judge you, ever. No, not now, or ever. This is the truth behind the truth. This is the word that cannot be spoken. This is the blasphemy of blasphemies. Judgment and Condemnation are among the Ten Illusions of Humans. They are simply not real.

11. Drop all expectations.

Nothing presents a bigger obstacle to long-lasting happiness (or, for that matter, *short-term* happiness) than expectations. Drop them immediately, and never entertain them again, about anyone or anything.

Forget about how you think things "should" be. There is no such thing as "should" in the universe. "Should" is a made-up human construction, having nothing to do with ultimate reality. Know that the twists and turns that remove us from the path that we thought we would be taking are not detours at all, but the fastest path from where we are to where we want to be—otherwise we wouldn't be taking it.

Trust that God knows what God is doing. Know that life is always conspiring in your favor. Understand that expectation is just your idea about something, and that this idea does not and cannot take into account the complex interweaving of life journeys undertaken by all of us, sequentially and simultaneously, in the co-creative and collective experience of the One Soul, expressed through the Many.

In other words, there is more going on here than meets the eye. There are more agendas than one. This is a single objective, but a multiple process.

Be constantly aware of that and you will find that holding onto expectations only puts a crimp in the Perfect Plan and the playing out of it on the stage of life by *all* the players.

What I am saying here is that expectations place a limit on the way you define perfection, and that this limit constricts your creation of perfection itself. Therefore, expect nothing, and take whatever you get. Embrace whatever shows up. Love what is.

Byron Katie wrote an extraordinary book a few years back called Loving What Is. *I adore it.*

12. Have compassion for yourself.

Don't make yourself "wrong" for any negative experience with which you may now be confronted (even if you feel you "deserve" it, or that you "brought it on yourself"—in fact, *especially* if you feel that way), but have compassion for yourself, and know that God has gifted you with the power inside of you to change yourself, your motives, your behaviors, your exterior conditions, and your life itself, *in the instant after this*.

Remember always that you are not your past, you are not who you were yesterday, nor even a moment ago. Let each new day, each new hour, each new moment mark a new beginning. Even if it is the last moment of your life, it is not too late to declare your new and grandest identity, and to claim it.

What I am saying here is that transformation is an instant-moment thing, open to us and available to us in any and every second. Life starts anew when you say it does. Therefore be gentle with yourself about yourself. Kiss away your (imagined) faults, foibles, and failings, and remember this always: If you saw you as God sees you, you would smile a lot.

13. Speak your truth as soon as you know it.

The biggest lesson I have learned in my life revolves around truth. There is no such thing as Absolute Truth in the objective sense, but there is subjective truth, there is *what is true for you*, and that is extraordinarily important in your life.

Seek to live authentically, seek to be fully you, for it is in living with only half of you showing, only half of you known, only half of you expressed, that unhappiness is guaranteed.

Do not hide your personal truth, your authentic feelings, your here-and-now experience from anyone—least of all from your dearest loved ones or your beloved other.

Interestingly, these are often the ones from whom we hide the most. Usually we do it because we do not want to hurt their feelings. Or, perhaps, because we do not want to lose them.

So we keep them in place by keeping them in doubt, by keeping them in the dark, by not telling them all of what is true for us. This is exactly the opposite of what we most benefit from doing, yet we live as a recluse from the expression of our own truest feelings, hopes, fears, and desires. And that is not living at all, that is dying.

The death is slow, but it is certain. And one morning we wake up and we simply no longer feel alive.

So tell your truth as soon as you know it. Do not think you are saving another person's feelings by holding back or holding in. A wonderful master once taught me: Speak your truth, but soothe your words with peace. You can share the most difficult truth gently. Do so. Do not think that by withholding your truth you are saving others from hurt. You are not. You are killing them softly with your song. And it is disingenuous and dishonest for you to do that.

What I am saying here is that the way to be happier than God is the way of truth. Tell the truth, to everyone about everything, then live your truth, in every moment and in every way, and you will be happy forever in your heart, for truth makes the spirit soar,

*truth sets the mind free, truth opens the heart, and truth
ignites the passion and releases the love of the soul.*

14. Watch the energies, catch the vibe.

Watch the energies around you. Listen to the
energies. Sense the vibe. These are the three levels of
reception. You can receive energies by seeing them,
by hearing them, and by feeling them.

The energy that you see is called *light*. The
energy that you hear is called *sound*. The energy that
you sense is called *feeling*.

Feeling is the language of the soul.

Pay attention to life's energies. At all times, you
are receiving them and you are sending them. Are
the energies you are sending resonating with the
energies you are receiving?

Happiness is the highest state of resonance.
This is exciting news, because this means that happiness is not something that falls on us from the sky,
but something that we can create.

To create happiness, simply create resonance
between the inside of you and the outside of you.
For instance, you can match the energy of the
clothes you wear with the mood you are in today. In
fact, you do this automatically. You can match the

energy of the food you eat with the energy of your body at any moment.

These are simple examples. Learn to listen to yourself. Feel the vibe of who you are, then do nothing and be with no one in an important way if the vibe does not match.

I can't go to a movie, I can't listen to music, I can't eat food or wear clothes or even say *words* or hold *thoughts*, with which I do not resonate.

You can *feel* these things. You can wave your hand over food and literally *feel* if it is good for you right now. You can feel people and spaces and colors and . . . and *everything*, if you just pay attention. Pay attention to your outer experience, and pay attention to inner experience. Make sure you are *in resonance* with the people, places, and things around you.

And *listen*. Just *listen*. Listening is a great art. Do you know that you can make people happy by just *listening to them?* Do you know that you can make yourself happy by listening to others? Listening is one of the richest ways of making love. It is rich with reward, rich with joy.

Try to absorb everything that is happening in your space. Then, see if there is a match. And slip out of the space if there is a mismatch.

What I am saying here is that when you follow this step you are much more likely to be happy. You need

*not "go along" just so you can "get along." Pay atten-
tion to the energy, catch the vibe, and if it resonates
with Who You Are and Who You Choose to Be, merge
with it and co-create with it. But if the energy and the
vibe are not in sync with Who You Are and Who You
Choose to Be, remove yourself from it. Not abruptly,
not rudely, not judgmentally, but gently, sweetly, softly,
kindly...and resolutely. Don't change your mind and
say, "Oh, well, I can put up with this . . ." Change your
experience.*

*Paying attention to the energies and the vibes of
life may cause you to change your diet, change your
reading habits, change what you watch on television
and at the movies, change what you wear, change the
way you talk . . . even change the company you keep.*

*Welcome these changes. They are the beginning
steps on the journey to joy.*

15. Smile.

This may sound silly, but it is one of the most
powerful devices I have ever come across. Every day,
smile five times for no good reason. And for certain
and for *sure*, smile broadly and immediately when
you *do* have a reason.

There are some people who never smile, or very rarely do. Even when a whole room is laughing, they cannot smile. These are people who may simply be self-conscious, or they may be deeply hurting. What it is important to know, however, is that smiling can heal both conditions. Smiling need not be merely a reaction. Smiling can be a deliberate, intentioned act. When it is that, it becomes an act of creation, and thus, a powerful tool.

Be quick to smile, and quick to share your smile with others. You will light up your heart and light up the room.

Several years ago I ran across a terrific book, *Smile for No Good Reason* by Lee L. Jampolsky. You will find it wonderful reading.

What I am saying here is to smile more! A smile actually changes the vibe of your body. It alters, physiologically, the chemistry of your being. It releases endorphins that have a health-giving effect. Did you know that? Check it out. It's medical science, and it's real.

16. Sing.

If you thought *that* sounded hokey, wait 'til you hear this!

Sing.

I want you to promise me that you will sing at least once each day. Promise me. It will change everything. *You cannot sing with a rotten disposition. And you cannot keep a rotten disposition when you sing.*

Sing in the shower every morning! Sing in the car! Sing softly in the ear of your lover. Sing out loud in the park. *Watch the place light up! Watch the smiles appear! Do you think that anyone can resist a person who is singing? Do you think the world can?*

Singing connects the mind with the heart and the heart with the soul. So *sing.* I dare you!

What I am saying here is that the tools and devices with which we can create happiness are so simple, so elegantly simple. And they are right in front of us. What are we talking about here? Giving. Watching. Listening. Feeling. Smiling. Singing. My God, this costs us nothing!

17. Know what to do when things are really bad.

Of course, there are times when things are really bad. No amount of positive thinking can change that. Things just are what they are. You can't cover it up, you can't pretend, you can't make it something other than it is.

What to do, what to do . . .

First, do not resist what is occurring. What you resist persists. This is going to sound strange . . . but bless it. Bless all the people and events that are disappointing you, that are besetting you, that are assailing you like so many arrows from afar.

Accept and receive the energy, because only then can you heal it. What you do not hold you cannot heal. Remember that always. What you do not hold, you cannot heal. So you must hold your experience, embrace it, engage it with loving kindness, bless it and *then* send it on its way.

Second, remember that exterior conditions cannot create interior conditions, ever. So, no matter *how* bad things get, the interior of you (your heart and soul and mind) cannot be affected by that which is exterior to you in any way except as you decide that it will.

You are still in charge of your own experience.

This is not some pie-in-the-sky, totally-out-of-reach ideal, this is something that many people have shown it is possible for all humans to do. The list of those who have endured enormous hardship and great difficulty in their life and still embraced a non-condemning, non-attacking, peaceful attitude is legend, and far too long to print here.

These are normal people, ordinary folks just like you and me. They maintained their equilibrium through physical pain, emotional injury, personal and professional defeat, and more. Earlier in this book I mentioned Nelson Mandela. He is but one example of what I'm talking about. Christopher Reeve, the actor whose skyrocketing career was brutally interrupted when he was thrown from his mount during a horse show and wound up totally paralyzed from the neck down, was another. There have been many more. How did they do it?

Somehow they reached back and found the courage within them to keep moving through the events with which they were confronted, to frame them in a new way in their minds, and thus to transform and shape their experience, turning it into something from which they could grow—and actually receive *benefit*.

My own life experience (I spent a year of my life living outside, in the weather, as a "street person," when I fell through the cracks of the social welfare system and was down to, quite literally, my last nickel) has taught me that the universe is a friendly place, that God is always on my side, and that I am never alone in facing the trials and turmoil of my life.

I have become very philosophical about life itself. I tell myself that all things happen for the highest good, and I believe it. I say two prayers that I just love. My first:

Dear God, I thank you today for that which is in my world and in my life. I rest my heart in the knowing that I will yet see pain turn into joy, sorrow into gladness, and even death into everlasting life.

My second:

Thank you, God, for helping me to understand that this problem has already been solved for me.

This may sound like I am a person who always keeps his cool, and I can assure you I am not. But I do know that I am on a journey here, a journey having nothing to do, in the end, with my body, and everything to do with my soul. And so I continue marching Homeward, understanding that every step along the way leads me to my eventual and ultimate and wonderful reunion with God, wherein which peace and joy and love without end resides.

What I am saying here is that God is with you, even unto the end of time. And when you experience the ever-present love of God, in you as you, you will be happier than you have ever been before.

CHAPTER 28

You Are Creating a Revolution

W e are on the verge of the most extraordinary and exciting tomorrow. It is a future undreamt of, precisely because it has *not* been dreamt of until now. It is the dreaming of it, quite literally the visioning of it in our minds, that will produce it. Until now, not nearly enough people have held this vision to pull it into creation. Now, all of that is changing.

A huge shift is taking place all across the earth. It is a shift in the way we see ourselves, in the way we experience ourselves, in the way we express ourselves as sentient beings. It is a movement away from our Old Thought that we must do as we have been told by Those In Charge, to a New Thought that *we* are Those In Charge.

This is the New Thought Movement, of which much has been written. This movement has been derided and ridiculed, made fun of and marginalized for years. Now it is emerging as the next great evolutionary leap for humankind.

The New Thought Movement is a *new way of thinking* about ourselves and about others, about life and about God. It is a new way of *using* our thinking as a tool in the creation of our reality.

Humanity has never thought of that before. Not humanity as a whole. Individuals have thought of this, of course. Throughout history there have been a handful of people, and even a few select groups, who have *thought of their thoughts* as the key to their future. But information about how to use the power of thought was closely held, closely guarded, and closely controlled by people of influence, lest it spread into the populace, shifting the balance of power from the hands of the few to the hands of the many.

Now, in these past 100 years or so (a blink of an eye in terms of our history on this planet), all of that has been changing—and the change has been like a snowball rolling downhill.

———

I said earlier that never before in this history of humankind has awareness of the Process of Personal Creation been so widespread. Now I want to add that the expansion of this awareness is not complete. Our collective understanding of it, our species' knowledge of it, is still growing, and it is growing exponentially. The progression is not 1-2-3-4-5. The progression is 2-4-8-16-32. When that rate of rapid information transfer occurs, *evolution* becomes *revolution.*

That is exactly what is happening right now, before our very eyes.

We who are alive in this extraordinary time are witnessing a revolution in humanity's consciousness, and in its experience of itself. In fact, we are creating it.

As I have noted here now on a number of occasions, critics of those who teach and use Personal Creation have decried the seemingly self-serving ways in which it is being touted and practiced. But these critics simply have no patience. *All* the great powers that humanity has discovered and unleashed have been used at *first* for lesser purposes, from fire to nuclear fission to thought power. It is built into the process of evolution itself that things move from the smaller to the grander.

Individuals will play with this new tool for a while, some of them indeed using it to create strictly self-serving outcomes. But give humanity a chance. Individual tinkering will soon produce collective applying of what will quickly be recognized as the most powerful force ever discovered by sentient beings.

Indeed, it will become clear that this is what it *means* to be sentient beings. It will at last be understood that "sentience" refers not simply to the faculty through which the external world is apprehended, *but through which it is created.*

———— ——— ————

It will not be lost on humanity that the most exciting aspect of Personal Creation is what it can do for the entire human race. Films such as *What the Bleep Do We Know?* and *The Secret*, books such as *The Law of Attraction* and the volume you are holding in your hand, have sent us a message about Who We Are and How Our World Works that has never before been so clearly articulated or so widely disseminated.

Soon everyone on the earth will know about all the great Principles of Life, how they work, the purpose for which they were created, and the potential they hold for changing the world.

And in those days it will come to pass that our Divinity will be revealed to us *by* us—and experienced by us *through* us. And the Unspoken Truth will be unspoken no more.

And that day will be blesséd indeed. For on that day we shall all be . . .

. . . *happier than God.*

AFTERWORD

If you would like to join a global community that seeks to use the Process of Personal Creation to bring peace to our planet and to spread and share the prosperity for all cultures and groups that peace will inevitably and finally produce, you are invited to explore the possibilities at:

www.nealedonaldwalsch.com

For more of the work of m. Claire, America's new young poetic voice, you may wish to visit:

www.mclairepoet.com

Blessings abide with all people,
and with you.

ADDENDUM

Following is an excerpt from the book *Communion with God* *that lists the* Ten Illusions of Humans *and the effect they have had on our lives.*

The Creator may be experienced and found within you and all around you. But you must look past The Illusions of Humans. You must ignore them.

Here are The Ten Illusions. Get to know them well, so that you will recognize them when you see them.

1. Need Exists
2. Failure Exists
3. Disunity Exists
4. Insufficiency Exists
5. Requirement Exists
6. Judgment Exists

7. Condemnation Exists
8. Conditionality Exists
9. Superiority Exists
10. Ignorance Exists

The first five of these are the Physical Illusions, having to do with life in your physical body. The second five are the Metaphysical Illusions, having to do with non-physical realities.

These are ten very impactful illusions which you created during the earliest part of your experience on Earth. There are hundreds of smaller ones that you create every day. Because you believe them, you have created a *cultural story* that has allowed you to enter into these Illusions and make them real.

You have, in fact, been doing this for a very long time.

A cultural story is a story which has been handed down from generation to generation, across centuries and millennia. It is the story that you tell yourself about yourself.

Because your cultural story is based on illusions, it produces myth, and not an understanding of reality.

The *Cultural Story of Humans* is that . . .

1. God has an agenda. *(Need Exists)*

2. The outcome of life is in doubt. *(Failure Exists)*

3. You are separate from God. *(Disunity Exists)*

4. There is not enough. *(Insufficiency Exists)*

5. There is something you have to do. *(Requirement Exists)*

6. If you do not do it, you will be punished. *(Judgment Exists)*

7. The punishment is everlasting damnation. *(Condemnation Exists)*

8. Love is, therefore, conditional. *(Conditionality Exists)*

9. Knowing and meeting the conditions renders you superior. *(Superiority Exists)*

10. You do not know that these are illusions. *(Ignorance Exists)*

This cultural story has been so ingrained in you that you now live it fully and completely. This, you tell each other, "is just the way it is."

You have been telling each other that now for many centuries. Indeed, for millennia after millennia. For so long, in fact, that myths have grown up around these illusions and stories. Some of the most prominent of these Myths have been reduced to concepts, such as . . .

- Thy will be done.

- Survival of the fittest.

- To the victor go the spoils.

- You were born in original sin.

- The wages of sin are death.

- Vengeance is Mine, sayeth the Lord.

- Ignorance is bliss. What you don't know won't hurt you.

- God only knows.

. . . and many others, equally destructive and non-serving.

Based on these illusions, stories and myths—none of which have anything to do with Ultimate Reality—here is how many humans have come to think about life:

"We are born into a hostile world, run by a God who has things He wants us to do and things He wants us not to do, and will punish us with everlasting torture if we don't get the two right.

"Our first experience in life is separation from our mother, the source of our life. This sets the tone and creates the context for our entire reality, which we experience to be one of separation from the source of *all* life.

"We are not only separate from all life, but from everything else *in* life. Everything that exists exists separate from us, and we are separate from everything else that exists. We do not want it this way, but this is the way it is. We wish it were otherwise, and, indeed, we strive for it to be otherwise.

"We seek to experience Oneness again with all things, and especially with each other. We may not know why, exactly, yet it seems almost instinctual. It feels like the natural thing to do. The only problem is, there does not seem to be enough of The Other to satisfy us. No matter what the Other Thing is that we want, we cannot seem to get enough of it.

"We cannot get enough love, we cannot get enough time, we cannot get money, we cannot get enough of whatever it is we think we need in order to be happy and fulfilled. The moment we think that we have enough, we decide that we want more.

"Since there is 'not enough' of whatever it is we think we need to be happy, we must 'do stuff' to get as much as we can get. Things are required of us to get everything, from God's love to the natural bounty of Life. Simply 'being alive' is not enough. Therefore WE, like all of life, *are not enough.*

"Because just 'being' isn't sufficient, there's stuff that we have to do. The ones who do the 'right stuff' get to have the things that they need to be happy. If you don't do the right stuff in the right way, you don't get to 'win.' Thus, the competition begins. There's 'not enough' out there, and so, we have to compete for it.

"We have to compete for everything, *including God.*

"This competition is tough. This is about our very survival. In this contest, only the fittest survive. Only to the victor go the spoils. If you are a loser, you live a hell on Earth, and after you die, if you are a loser in the competition for God, you experience hell again—this time forever.

"Death was actually created by God because our forebears made the wrong choices. Adam and Eve had everlasting life in the Garden of Eden, but then, Eve ate the fruit of the tree of the Knowledge of Good and Evil, and she and Adam were driven from the garden by an angry God, who sentenced them, *and all their progeny forevermore*, to death as The First Punishment. Henceforth, life in the body would be limited, and no longer everlasting, and so would the *stuff* of life.

"Yet God will give us back our everlasting life if we never again break His rules. God's love is unconditional; it is only God's rewards which are not. God loves us even as He condemns us to everlasting damnation. It hurts Him more than it hurts us, because He really wants us to return home, but He can't do anything about it if we misbehave. The choice is ours.

"The trick is, therefore, to not misbehave. We need to live a good life. We must strive to do so. In order to do so, we have to know the truth about what God wants and does not want from us. We cannot please God, we cannot avoid offending Him, if we do not know Right from Wrong. So we have to know the Truth about that.

"The Truth is simple to understand and easy to know. All we have to do is listen to the prophets, the teachers, the sages, and the source and founder of our religion. If there is more than one religion, and therefore, more than one source and founder, then we have to make sure to pick the Right One. Picking the Wrong One could result is us being a Loser.

"When we pick the Right One, we are superior, we are better than our peers, because we have The Truth on our side. This state of being 'better' allows us to claim most of the other prizes in the contest without actually contesting them. We get to declare ourselves the Winner in the competition *before the competition begins.* It is out of this awareness that we give ourselves all the advantages, and write the Rules of Life in such a way that certain others find it nearly impossible to win the really big prizes.

"We do not do this out of meanness, but simply in order to ensure that our victory is guaranteed—as rightly it should be, since it is those of our religion, of our nationality, of our race, of our gender, of our political persuasion, who know The Truth, and therefore deserve to be Winners.

"Because we deserve to win, we have a right to threaten others, to fight with them, and to kill them if necessary, in order to produce this result.

"There may be another way to live, another thing that God has in mind, another, larger Truth, but if there is, we don't know it. In fact, it is not clear whether we are even *supposed* to know it. It is possible that we are not supposed to even try to know it, much less to truly know and understand God. To try is to be presumptuous, and to declare that you have actually done so is to blaspheme.

"God is the Unknown Knower, the Unmoved Mover, the Great Unseen. Therefore, we cannot know the truth *that we are required to know* in order to meet the conditions *that we are required to meet* in order to receive the love *that we are required to receive* in order to avoid the condemnation *that we are seeking to avoid* in order to have the everlasting life *that we had before any of this started.*

"Our ignorance is unfortunate, but should not be problematical. All we need do is take what we think we *do* know—our cultural story—on faith, and proceed accordingly. This we have tried to do, each according to his or her own beliefs, out of which we have produced the life that we are now living, and the reality on Earth that we are creating.

"This is how most of the human race has it constructed. You each have your minor variations, but this is, in essence, how you live your lives, justify your choices, and rationalize your outcomes.

"Some of you do not accept all of this, yet all of you accept some of it. And you accept these statements as the Operating Reality not because they reflect your innermost wisdom, *but because someone else has told you that they are true.*

"At some level, you have had to make yourself believe them.

"This is called Make Believe."

None of this is real.

— *Communion with God*
by Neale Donald Walsch
Putnam, 2000